Reaching for
the Moon

Reaching
for the
MOON

on Asian
Religious
Paths

Kenneth W. Morgan

Anima

LIBRARY OF CONGRESS
Library of Congress Cataloging-in-Publication Data

Morgan, Kenneth W., 1908-
    Reaching for the moon : on Asian religious paths / Kenneth W. Morgan.
        p.   cm.
    Includes bibliographical references (p.   ).
    ISBN 0-89012-059-5 :
    1. Spiritual life. 2. Asia—Religious life and customs.
    I. Title.
    BL624.M665 1990
    291 .095—dc20   90-751
                                                                        CIP

The Goto Museum in Tokyo has graciously given permission to reproduce Hakuin's *Monkey Reaching for the Moon on the Water*.

Excerpts from the *Tao te Ching* have been reprinted with permission of Macmillan Publishing Company from *The Way of Lao Tzu* translated by Wing-Tsit Chan. Copyright © 1985 by Macmillan Publishing Company.

Printed in USA

Contents

Foreword

Reaching for the Moon

Hakuin's *Monkey Reaching For The Moon*, now treasured in Tokyo's Goto Museum, suggests that followers of a religious path reach for, but never firmly grasp the good and the sacred they see reflected in the world. Hakuin's moon reflected on the water is a Zen circle, a symbol that can be correctly drawn only by an enlightened seeker who has attained satori, who has become aware of reality that is seen as sacred.

For more than half a century I have been observing how followers of Asian religious paths respond to what they see as true, as good, and as sacred in the realities they experience in this ever-changing, puzzling world. The realities they see as given without regard for human preferences include their consciousness of their natural environment, and of birth and death, love and hate, pain, sorrow and happiness; and revelations, enlightenment, heavens, hells, superhuman beings, divine judgments and rewards, souls, karma, rebirth, transmigration. Followers of each path tell us how to live in harmony with what they hold to be true, with what is recognized as good, and with the

Sacred that has been discovered in the realities of human existence.

The most dependable guides along the different religious ways I have observed were the ones who have been moved to follow their path by the wonder, gratitude, awareness, and awe that center their attention outside themselves, guides who are trying to live in closer harmony with what they see is true, is good, is sacred.

Sympathetic study of religious ways other than one's own helps religious seekers to see the realities of their own path more clearly, to discover new ways for humans to increase the good in their relations with each other and with the natural world, and to gain new understanding of the Sacred. This is true for Asians looking at other Asian or African or European or American religious ways, as well as for those who start from non-Asian backgrounds. Such seekers may be moved to turn back to re-examine their own way when they observe that most people continue on the religious path they started to follow in their childhood.

Once in Malaysia I met a Buddhist nun who was the stimulating and caring head of a clinic for needy children. Her eyes glowed as she said she counts it her good fortune that she was born this time where she could grow up knowing the truths taught by the Buddha. Not long before that I had been visiting with a Muslim businessman in southern India who was giving half his time to raising funds for a school for orphan children and to helping administer the services of the mosque for the neediest in their community. It was the fasting period known as Ramadan, he had just finished his devotions and he smiled as he told me how fortunate he was to have been born into a Muslim family, particularly into a Shi'i family which taught him the joy of reciting the words of Ali after chanting the *Qur'an*, for ''it is Ali who most truly warms our hearts and opens our eyes.'' Somehow, both were fortunate, as were many children in Kuala Lumpur and Madras.

What we are told is true, and good, and sacred in

human experience has come to us through persons who were born into particular cultures and shaped by traditions accepted or rejected. We choose more wisely between what is taught by followers of different religious paths when we know something of the background and experiences that have shaped their evaluations of our human situation. Since I am here making judgments about the realities we all share, and some of these may be illusions or prejudices, a sketch of my background may make it easier to detect and avoid slips I make.

The speculative judgments offered here are the reflections of a man who was born into a devout Methodist home in the Middle West of the United States, who was graduated from a Protestant-supported college in Ohio, then spent several years in graduate study of philosophy and religion at Harvard University. While I was in graduate school, I checked what I was learning about religion by observing services in a variety of Protestant and Catholic churches and Jewish synagogues where I gained new insights concerning ritual, interpretation of scriptures, social obligations, prayer, devotion, and awareness of the sacred.

As I was trying to find some reconciling order in what religious people claimed to be centrally important in a religious way of life, it occurred to me that I was considering only my own Jewish and Christian traditions as they have been modified by the Greek and Roman and European cultures in which they have existed for some centuries. What of Asia? What of the religious insights and practices Asians have accepted? Could I make discoveries by observing Hindus in their home culture, just as I had in observing New England Protestants, Roman and Greek and Russian Catholics, and Jews in Boston? These questions led me to India, in 1935, to live in Ramakrishna Mission ashrams, conversing at length with the Swamis and their friends, studying the *Bhagavad Gita* with their guidance, experimenting with various meditative disciplines, and reading Plato, the Bible, *Theologia Germanica*, *The Imitation of Christ*, Augustine's *Confessions*, and sometimes in the evening, Shakespeare.

During the second world war, I was on the staff of the American Friends Service Committee in the conscientious objector program for pacifists. After the war, influenced by what I had learned from religious ways other than those of my boyhood, I became a Quaker.

For more than a quarter of a century I was at Colgate University, first as a chaplain, then as a professor of religion. In addition to teaching, I directed the endowed Fund for the Study of the Great Religions, encouraging undergraduate courses in Asian religions and helping teachers of such courses have opportunities to study in Asia. I also created and managed Chapel House, a center for religious study, devotions, and meditation. It provided a chapel, books, works of art, and recorded music from many religious traditions for anyone from anywhere in the world who wanted to take the initiative to continue a religious search there, for a few hours, or days, or weeks.

I returned to Asia several times to gather materials for books designed to introduce students to Hinduism, Buddhism, and Islam as seen by followers of those religious paths. I first prepared an outline of what I thought should be covered in such a book, then I went to Asia to interview religious scholars recognized there as outstanding in their tradition, modifying the outline in the light of their suggestions and then commissioning the writing by scholars who were recommended by their co-religionists. Those extended interviews with Hindus, Buddhists, and Muslims about their beliefs and practices, together with the experience of teaching Asian religious ways to alert and inquiring students in America, provide the background for asking here what I have learned from religious ways other than those of my childhood.

In my attempts to understand religious ways and to encourage the study of religious paths other than one's own, I have admired and learned from men and women who are Buddhist: Theravada or Mahayana, Tibetan, Japanese, Chinese, Vietnamese, Burmese, Sri Lankan, and Thai. From Orthodox, Reform, and Conservative Jews—Zionist and non-Zionist. From English, American, Irish, Italian, and German Roman Catholics, and from Greek and Russian Orthodox Catholics. From Hindus who are Saivites, Vaishnavites, or devotees of God in other forms. From Protestants—particularly Anglican, Presbyterian, Quaker, and Methodist. From Shi'i and Sunni Muslims, in many variations from Morocco to Indonesia. From Sikhs and Jains and followers of the teachings of the Tao, of Confucius, and of Shinto. Some of them say that all paths lead to God, or that we are all climbing the same mountain and will meet at the top. Others say theirs is the only Way. But when I explore Asian religious ways I find that often I am only in the foothills, with some bypaths that are dead ends, some valleys shadowed with tangled undergrowth—and that there are also many beckoning paths, often arduous, leading to awesome peaks, some hidden in clouds.

When I reflect on my efforts to understand Asian religious ways I find that I have been looking for followers of religious paths—contemporary, or remembered for their writings, music, works of art, or compassionate acts—who are committed to live by what seems to them to be true, who recognize some given aspects of their world as good and some of the good as sacred. I have searched for people of sensitive awareness who respond to the world with wonder and joyous appreciation for the beauty and diversity they see, with awe for the mysteries not fully grasped, and with compassionate help for the needy and suffering. I have found such persons in each religious group.

What seems to be true, and what of that seems to be good, I take only as tentative informed opinion, established by observations and by the conclusions drawn from them. I have learned to be content with truths that are open to revision again and again, but are the best known at the moment. I find I have more confidence in judgments that are in agreement with persons I admire for the insights, integrity, and compassion revealed in their actions. Such agreement is reassuring, but it may lead to the uncritical adoption of errors the admired persons have made, just as the discovery of disagreement may reveal my own errors of judgment.

In the twentieth century, new ease of transportation and communication have brought about an unprecedented intermingling of cultures that brings together followers of quite different religious paths, some of whom share their insights concerning what is true, good, sacred. What follows is an account of such sharing of religious insights and of some of the problems faced when followers of different religious paths come together as friends. Here, the spelling of words and transliterations associated with a path, and the capitalization of titles, names, or words used with a sense of honor or reverence, conform to preferences expressed by followers of that path.

One

Beginning the Journey

In the early nineteen-thirties, when as a graduate student in philosophy and religion I asked a visiting lecturer from India some questions about Hindu religious ways, he suggested that I seek out a friend of his, a young Swami who had recently come to the United States representing the Ramakrishna Mission. A few weeks later, when Swami Nikhilananda came to Boston, we spent a warm spring afternoon sitting on the bank of the Charles River talking about what Hindus believe and do. I remember sitting there thinking how remarkable it was to be in Cambridge talking with a man for whom whatever is happening in the lives of the Bostonians around us— the people rowing on the river, lolling on the bank, driving by in cars, in their rooms studying—is shaped by karma; marveling that, for him, they had been born by transmigrating from a previous life and would be born again and again in the future with their health, their thoughts, desires, actions, joys, sorrows, and rebirths controlled by the causal continuity of karma. The realities of his world had never even been mentioned in my educational and religious upbringing. He spoke of God with unself-conscious assurance, using names unfamiliar to me, quoting the *Gita*, as he called it, to support his statements, and giving equal authority to the teachings of Ramakrishna, his revered Bengali Master, who died in 1886.

During the next two years, after several more conversations with Swami Nikhilananda and some intensive study, I decided to go to India for a year to learn about Hinduism from people for whom it is a way of life. I wanted to see whether contemporary Hinduism had been accurately presented in the available books written by Europeans and Americans, to see what it would be like to live with people who looked upon me as unclean and would not allow me to enter their temples or kitchens because I would pollute them—people who looked on my religion as inferior, as a deficient view of reality. I wanted to see whether I could forget color and social distinctions, and I wanted to experiment with meditative disciplines in an environment that did not require any creedal or ritual conformity. I had been told that in the Ramakrishna Mission ashrams in India all they would require of me would be that I did not ask for any special privilege and did not bother anyone. Swami Nikhilananda arranged for me to be admitted to an ashram in Bombay with the understanding that if all went well there in the first weeks, they would recommend me to the other ashrams wherever I wanted to go in India.

In 1935 I moved from an academic community in Cambridge to a Hindu ashram in Bombay, survived the pass/fail examination there, and went on to ashrams at Calcutta, Varanasi, Vrindavan, and to the Himalayas for an extended stay at Almora and Mayavati. As I became acquainted with the Swamis—there were from three or four to more than fifty in the different ashrams—one of my earliest impressions was that they were as varied as the Priests, Ministers, and Rabbis I had been observing in America. Some of the Swamis were simply marking time, escaping from the world, some were kindly and hard-working servants of the ashram, caring for the grounds or working in the kitchen or dispensary or school, some were recluses. Among them were Swamis who were unself-consciously aware of a sacred quality infusing their lives, revealed in their devotions and in their wise and compassionate caring for their fellow humans and their environment.

A few days after I was settled in Belur Math in Calcutta, one of the Swamis timidly suggested to me that although the ashram did not serve breakfast, some of the weaker brethren were accustomed to gather back of the kitchen early in the morning for a cup of tea and a chappaty, and I would be welcome. I was pleased to see, the next morning, that most of the Swamis were there and a goodly number of them liked to sit around to chat for half an hour or so after eating. They asked me many questions about life in America and American attitudes toward India, which encouraged me to ask them about what they believed and how they put their beliefs into practice. There I was, fresh out of graduate school, and my carefully formulated questions again and again sent a ripple of chuckles through my Swami friends, surprised that I could misunderstand and be ignorant of so many aspects of Indian beliefs and customs. It was back of the kitchen of a Hindu ashram in Calcutta that I first saw some of my preconceptions about religious ways, preconceptions carefully shaped in academically acceptable forms, fall by the wayside. That they fell to the accompaniment of warm laughter of friends made it easier.

After several of the breakfast sessions, one of the Swamis invited me to go with him to Kalighat, a major Hindu pilgrimage place where one of the rituals performed is sacrifice to the Goddess Kali, the ceremonial beheading of goats which then can be eaten by orthodox Bengali Hindus. The first three goats killed must be given to the priests—after that, only the head is given to the priests to be sold, and the rest of the goat can be taken home by the donor for a feast. Once started, a dozen or so were quickly killed by placing the head of the goat in a forked stanchion so the priest could sever the neck with a quick blow of a sharp curved knife.

As we walked around the temple compound we saw a priest who sat by a smoldering fire and was occasionally hired to make a fire-offering for a devotee who had been neglecting that ritual, or felt incompetent to perform it properly. We watched the young men doing a profitable business noisily hawking their floral wreaths to be placed on the images in the temple. I could not enter the temple because, my Swami friend explained, as a non-Hindu I am impure since I have not observed the practices nor performed the rituals necessary for purification and therefore would, in the opinion of many devotees, pollute the sacred place and make it necessary to expend a great deal of effort and large sums for rituals of purification before the shrine could be used again for worship. I could, however, stand outside and watch the people. I was impressed by their ability to ignore all the noise and distractions in the courtyard, and by their unself-conscious devotion as they worshiped Kali.

As we wandered around the temple precincts and down to the bathing ghats we were joined by a priest who was a friend of the Swami: it was the first time I had heard anyone call out "Brahman" to warn lower caste persons to get out of the way so no unclean shadow would fall on a Brahman. (This the Swami explained later with an indulgent smile, aware that I, an untouchable, had been walking beside the priest as he called.)

When I asked about the rows of beggars, the Swami said they were expecting to be fed by people who had vowed to come to Kalighat and feed beggars if their prayers were granted. As an example, he said, a man whose child was ill might pray to Kali that if the child recovered he would make a pilgrimage to Kalighat and there as a sign of his gratitude would provide a feast for one hundred beggars. Then, if the child did recover, the father would make the pilgrimage, often a journey of many days, and at the temple ask the priests to provide a feast for a hundred beggars. He might give the priest a hundred rupees (which at that time was a small fortune and could leave the devotee deeply in debt) so each beggar could have several curries and a generous serving of rice, sweets, and fruit, in order that Kali would know how grateful he was.

Now, the Swami explained, the priests are greedy men. Kalighat is such a profitable temple, and there had been so much competition for the priestly control of the shrine, that it was finally divided among four families to share the income equally. The priest would praise the devotee for his generosity and then would probably give one hundred beggars a cup of rice and a small serving of curry. When I asked whether the donor would be indignant, the Swami replied that the man gave a rupee for each beggar because he knew the priest would keep so much that unless he gave generously the beggars would get almost nothing. He did, however, expect the priest to perform correctly the rituals of gratitude before the image of Kali, and if that had been neglected there would have been serious trouble. A priest, said the Swami, is simply a technician who knows how to perform rituals correctly, and one should expect that quite often technicians, whether they be priests, doctors, lawyers, or mechanics, would overcharge.

I was new to India, and Kalighat gave me more questions than answers that day. How important is ritual to a religious way of life, and how can we judge between rituals? Is purity a relevant religious concern? Do you feed the poor in order to impress the Deity? Are the religious professionals, whatever they may be called, only skillful religious mechanics? I knew the Swami had received a degree from Calcutta University before becoming a Swami, that he was a sophisticated scholar of religion, and I suspected that he had brought me to Kalighat in order to teach me something about Hinduism, so I timidly asked him whether he could worship at Kalighat.

He sighed, and said he had hoped I would have understood by that time. As he talked I sensed that he had spent the day with me at Kalighat because he thought my comments in the morning sessions behind the kitchen at Belur Math showed that I did not understand *adhikara:* he thought a day at Kalighat might help me to see that religious choices are always determined by the level of religious competence the devotee has attained. He patiently explained that when he worshiped at Kalighat as a boy his competence made it perfectly fitting for him, just as it was for all the people around us, but that now he finds other ways of worshiping more appropriate because his level of religious competence has changed. Adhikara, the Swami said, is one of the given realities of human existence (like sleeping and waking): our reactions to the Holy, the Sacred, are determined by the level of competence we have attained, a level that may go up or down according to varying circumstances. Some persons can see almost nothing that could be called divine, some with little competence have distorted vision, and some people have attained amazing wisdom. He encouraged me to relax and observe the level of competence of individuals—but without making comparative judgments like a professor grading papers from A to F, without judging any person's religious competence to be higher than another's, or using one's own level of competence as a measure for comparing others.

After several weeks in ashrams I stopped for a few days at the college Rabrindranath Tagore founded, Santiniketan, hoping to learn what they taught about Hinduism. I had no idea that a wandering graduate student might meet the famous poet, but the first morning when the professor who was showing me around discovered that I was being shadowed by the British secret police (who had arrested me in Calcutta because I had talked with Indians who were suspected of advocating independence), he rushed off to tell the Master. Evidently the fact that I was being watched by a man from the Criminal Investigation Division was a good recommendation, for Tagore immediately invited me to visit him. He was living in a little house he had built to demonstrate that a house made of the local clays available even to the poorest could be gracefully proportioned, beautified with bas-reliefs by the door, and adequate for the simple needs of a family.

He talked of the college and expressed his pleasure that the village work carried on by the Santiniketan students and faculty had been the inspiration for Gandhi's village reform program—for Gandhi could, with his persuasive charm, spread it throughout India. He spoke enthusiastically about the beauty of the flat Bengali plain where the distant horizon can be seen, where individual trees stand out against the sky in all their beauty and variety, not lost in the green mass of a forest, and where the constantly changing clouds are seen as mountains ever new in color and shape. He talked spontaneously of his wonder at the beauty and variety in the world around him in the trees and flowers and sky, and in the students and faculty and the villagers nearby—and of the ways such wonders might be seen and fostered.

Tagore was eager to find more effective ways to move toward political freedom in India. He was confident it would come, but in 1935 we could not see how or when. He had recently returned from a visit to the Soviet Union where he was most impressed by the great increase in literacy. He said that before the revolution eighty-five percent of the Russians were illiterate and now only fifteen percent could not read: he hoped that India would soon go through a similar revolution, for no price would be too great to pay to make the people of India literate. When I pointed out that such a revolution in India might mean that thousands of people would be killed, he said that India could afford the loss of millions of people for that goal. When I suggested that it would mean the destruction of organized Hinduism, he replied that Hinduism was rife with superstitions that should be washed away, after that the temples could be rebuilt, and in the end true religion would not suffer because the Indian people are the most spiritual in the world and true religious life would inevitably be restored after they had learned to read and write.

It surprised me to hear from Rabindranath Tagore the familiar generalization that the Indian people are the most spiritual in the world. In my limited experience in the few weeks I had been in India, as I came to know some Indians well I was finding my new Hindu friends to be as varied—as selfish or as selfless, as kindly or as passively unconcerned, as indifferent or as compassionately aware—as any people I had known. Tagore, who in our conversation had quite unself-consciously expressed his wonder at the beauties of the Bengali earth and sky, his compassionate concern for human beings, and his passionate desire to bring more beauty, justice, and harmony to the world, stood out as a remarkable and challenging example of what an admirable religious person a follower of the path of the Hindus might become. His comment that he belonged to a religious community of people who, more than all others, are attuned to the sacred realities, seemed incongruous to me.

And as I puzzled over what Tagore said about the price India should gladly pay for a revolution that would bring literacy, I saw more clearly that, if the real world includes human beings with selves transmigrating from existence to existence in a just, karmic continuity, the transmigration of some millions of selves might not be seen as an enormous tragedy. Then I remembered what the good Swami had been trying to teach me about adhikara, that it is an accurate description of reality to say that humans rise to the level of religious competence they are capable of attaining on the basis of previous experience. If Tagore accepted adhikara as an accurate description of the way humans inevitably react, then if the superstitions which hinder true knowledge of reality were wiped out, it would be possible through literacy for the truths known in India about the Gods and human existence to be more widely known and thus many more humans would rise to higher levels of religious competence.

While I was still uneasy about Tagore's comment that the Indians are the most spiritual people in the world (was it just a casual remark? was it irony? did he mean it?), I chanced to meet a young British professor who was teaching social sciences in a missionary school. In response to my question as to how a man with his superior academic training from a renowned English university happened to be teaching in a small mission school in India he replied that because of the depression in England there had been no position for him and this job had made it possible for him to get married, to have a house with servants, and to teach in his field. He had not been much of a Christian when he came out, he said, but he was grateful for his opportunity because here he had become a Christian—perhaps influenced by the sincere devotion of the missionaries, but chiefly from the experience of teaching bright and enquiring Hindu and Muslim students. They used to come up after class to discuss religious ideas and would ask, "What do you Christians have that we don't have?" He would give them the best answers he could and the next day they would be back with quotations and examples to show they had that too. This went on for some time until one day he thought of how he could beat them: he told them that as a Christian he had Jesus Christ, and since there was only one Jesus Christ, they could not claim they had that too. He said the realization that Jesus Christ was unique made him a Christian.

It seemed to me that his students had asked, and he had tried to answer, the wrong question. Instead of making comparisons designed to show that one religious way is better than another, they might have gained new insights about their inherited religious traditions, and better understanding of religious ways other than their own, if they had asked each other, "What do you accept as true, as good, as sacred—and how do you know?"

On that first trip to India, I lived for a time in the Ramakrishna Mission ashram and hospital in Varanasi [it was called Banaras then] not far from the Ganges. Day after day I observed the ritual practices of Hindu devotees at the ghats on the banks of by the Ganges, and at nearby temples, trying to understand what the rituals meant to them. At nearby Sarnath, where the Buddha preached his first sermon setting in motion "the Wheel of the Dharma," I saw Buddhist pilgrims from Sri Lanka, India, and Tibet amicably using quite different rituals side by side with great devotion.

In 1935, at the new Sarnath temple being built by Sri Lankan Buddhists, I found a pamphlet discussing the *Origins of Christianity* as seen from the perspective of "A Buddhist Student of the Hebrew Bible":

The alleged teachings of Jesus as recorded in the Four Gospels have to be analysed. His sayings may be divided into two categories: the Good and the Bad. . . . He advocated poverty, prayer, fasting, and preached a God with human attributes. His teachings were intended for the ignorant, illiterate and the poor. He believed that the rich will go to hell, and the poor to heaven. . . . The wealthy man was to him like a red rag to a bull. In cursing the fig tree, when he knew that it was not the season for bearing figs, his angry temperament was exhibited. . . . He proclaimed an ascetic ethic; but he was a wine bibber and went about eating and drinking. . . . No moral reformer ever gave people to drink intoxicants; but the first miracle which he wrought was to convert water into wine which feat after all was very elementary in the science of thaumaturgy. . . . He was always on the lookout for food. Boiled fish was His favorite. Even after the resurrection the first thing He wanted was some fish to eat. It was a step from the sublime to the ridiculous. . . . Jesus could get only twelve disciples to follow him and they were illiterate. . . . He preached a horrible unsocial ethic which happily is not carried out by any one today. He said: "He that loveth father or mother more than me is not worthy of me. . . ." The Buddha elevated parenthood to its sublimest point, accentuating with emphasis filial gratitude of the supremest kind which the son has to show to his parents whom He compared to Brahma, the ·loving God, chief of the Devas. . . . Chinese and Aryan morality emphasises filial piety as a supreme duty. It was for this reason that Jesus lost his place in the hearts of the people of Asia who are ever tolerant towards religious founders; it was for this reason that his creed became unacceptable in Asia.[1]

Once, many years later, when I asked my students to comment on that quotation, a Conservative Jewish student, an able young man with an open mind, sincerely puzzled, said that he had read most of the New Testament since coming to college, had lived among Christian students for many years, and he could see nothing in the quotation to which a Christian could take exception. Some of the Christian students were amused by the discovery that a Theravada Buddhist could speak of Christianity with condescension; others were a bit troubled by the suggestion that a religious person could be criticized for being angry, or for having a God with human attributes. Christians who take exception to derogatory comments about Jesus and the teachings recorded in the Four Gospels may sense something of the reactions Theravadans have when they read many of the writings about Theravada Buddhism by Christians, or by Muslims, and even by Mahayana Buddhists.

When I was first in India, some of the Swamis where I was living urged me to visit Gandhi at his ashram in Wardha. At the ashram I found that he would routinely give visitors from abroad a few minutes for a chat, so I decided to ask him a question that I hoped he would want to discuss more fully than he could in five minutes. I waited my turn and late in the afternoon was ushered in as the last of the visitors. He had only spoken a few words when I realized why he was having so much influence on those who met him: he had a natural, spontaneous charm that gave the impression that his day up to that moment had been

only ordinary, but now he was thoroughly enjoying himself. It did not seem to be a device, a manipulation of his
guest; he was sincere, open, almost childlike. I introduced
myself as a graduate student in religious studies now living
in ashrams in India and learning what I could about Hinduism with the intention of returning to the United States
where I would be meeting with students from time to time.
I said that occasionally students would tell me they had
never been interested in any religious concerns but recently they have come to admire very much an older man or
woman who is the kind of person they would like to be, and
they have discovered, when they asked, that the actions of
the person admired have been shaped by trust in God. But,
the students will say, they do not believe or trust in God,
nor see how anyone can, and they will ask: "How can that
knowledge and trust be found?" What, I asked Gandhi,
should I say to such students? Gandhi smiled and said that
his schedule was full for the rest of the afternoon, but he
invited me to stay at the ashram overnight so he would
have ample time the next morning to answer the question.

I stayed overnight and slept on the roof—and it was
cold! I ate the supper of pounded rice and vegetables and
listened to Gandhi's explanation that he had experimented
with many diets in India, England, and Africa, and had
discovered that what we eat makes us what we are: that to
eat eggs makes us chicken-brained, and to eat pork makes
us like pigs. In the end he had concluded that the healthi-
est diet, the diet best for the religious life, is food similar to
what he had as a boy in Rajkot State. We went to the evening worship service for the ashram community: first a
chant, then a passage from the *Bhagavad Gita*, then chanting again, then a quotation from the *Qur'an*, followed by
singing a verse from a Christian hymn, and a final chant.
On the way back to the central ashram building we passed
the home of an eight-year-old boy who had been at the
worship service and had been chattering with Gandhi as
we walked. Gandhi stopped at the gate and told him it was

time for him to go to bed, and when the boy dropped down to kiss Gandhi's foot in farewell suddenly Gandhi reached down and playfully rolled him over in the dust, saying, "only once, you rascal!" "No! No! Bapuji, three times!" But Gandhi picked him up and pushed him through the gate telling him that of course it would be only once—for one kiss would be a mark of respect for an ordinary man, but three would be for a holy man.

Gandhi said the religious search begins with dedication to truth—without that, nothing happens. The search will of necessity involve asceticism in order that one's body and mind may be completely controlled, may not interfere with the search. This may require fasting and being hard on oneself, but the things abandoned will not be regretted any more than one regrets the fingernail or the hair clipped off. Asceticism only cuts off those things that interfere with the search for truth. Gandhi pointed out a young man at the ashram who had recently been in prison with him and there had started his search for God which was continuing at Wardha. He was eating only raw vegetables, that day it was soy beans soaked in cold water; often he had only two hours of sleep, and he would discipline his body by sleeping while standing up to his waist in water. He spent his time chanting, singing, and repeating his mantra.

Gandhi said the motive power for social activity and for seeking knowledge comes from meditative practices. There must be a minimum of an hour a day in individual meditation; and we must also join regularly with others in worship, because group chanting (of mantras and passages of scripture) and group singing are necessary for strengthening resolves and enlightening religious understanding. Some time should be spent in the study of religious writings—a study which will become more valuable as the seeker progresses in the control of the body and mind through physical disciplines and meditation He found the *Bhagavad Gita* the most useful for study, particularly the second chapter which, he said, was the basis for all his thoughts and actions.

Gandhi emphasized particularly the connection between meditation and the search for truth. Meditation requires that the seeker sit in a posture that can be maintained for hours without difficulty, such as the lotus posture, so that the body does not distract and the mind can be stilled. When, in meditation, the body and the mind have become tranquil, the attention is centered an a mantra to be repeated over and over, hour after hour, day after day. With a proper mantra, that practice will eventually, inevitably bring the seeker to an awareness of God and to an overwhelming trust in God. Ordinarily it would take about nine years of such discipline and meditation, eight hours or more a day, but it might take twelve years; for some it may come in less time, but it will require discipline and years of effort to learn to trust God.

The best mantra to use, he said, is OM. A mantra, of course, has the power to transform the person who repeats it properly and to link that person with the divine. OM is particularly useful, Gandhi said, because when you say it properly you open your mouth and begin by bringing the deepest sound possible up from your diaphragm and continuing as the sound rises in pitch until it is coming from your lips and teeth—thus you have said all sounds. Names are simply combinations of those sounds, so you have said all names, have said the names of everything that exists. As you go on repeating the mantra OM day after day, year after year, your mind is directed to its true meaning and power and you are inevitably led to God.

Such was Gandhi's instruction for those who ask how to be aware of God and how to trust the God of that awareness.

After several months in ashrams in cities of North India, I spent the next six months in the Ramakrishna Mission ashram in the Himalayas, not far from the western border of Nepal. There I lived alone, about five minutes walk from the main building, with opportunities for long conversations with the Swamis after the noon meal which we took together. We discussed karma, transmigration, mantra, yoga, gurus, rituals, meditation, avataras, the *Vedas*, and particularly the *Bhagavad Gita*—and, of course, how and when India might be free from the embarrassments and agonies of colonialism.

They had little to say about Muslims or Buddhists, and often dismissed Indian Christians as people who had moved to Christianity to escape from caste or to get an education or a job under the British raj. One of the Swamis had read and re-read *The Imitation of Christ*, substituting Krishna whenever Christ appeared in the text, and treasured it as a guide to meditation.

Another Swami had been an active member of a group of young Bengalis engaged in violent opposition to the British, then had come to the Ramakrishna Mission to become a Swami, in order to avoid creating any more bad karma through violence or hatred, and to live in a way that would develop good karmic forces shaping his future transmigrations. One of the Swamis gave most of his time to running a dispensary for the mountain people who had no medical services. He had studied ways to treat the malaria they brought up from the plains, to set broken bones, to care for wounds if mauled by a tiger, to relieve suffering from burns, and often had more than a hundred patients a day. Then, one day, he closed the dispensary and went down to an ashram near Bombay to spend all his time practicing austerities, in order that he might end this existence without carrying binding karmic results into his next birth. It was a couple of months of turning away dozens of ill and injured patients before another Swami was found to open the dispensary—and everyone who talked about the Swami who had gone away praised him for choosing the nobler, and harder way, the way that leads to salvation from the round of transmigrations.

One day, when we were chatting after the noon meal, I asked the Swamis a question that had been raised for me by a conversation in Lucknow earlier that year. In the dining room of the hotel there I had met an American, an agricultural specialist from Wisconsin, in India on an experimental project supported by Jawaharlal Nehru to try to increase the production of wheat in the northern provinces. He had no previous experience in India but he assured me that farmers are the same everywhere, reluctant to change, but willing to adopt new methods shown to be profitable. He had gone to a village and persuaded one villager to join him in experimenting with the wheat crop. They made a small metal plow that could cultivate deeper than was customary, used the fertilizer and the seed he provided and their crop was so good that the villager could pay for the seed and fertilizer for that year and the next, and still have enough to support his family for a year and to build a new house. I was excited by the story of what they had accomplished and thought it was the first step toward producing enough food to free the Indians from hunger. But he said I should not expect such results: the increased production was attracting more monkeys to the fields and since the farmers would not kill the monkeys, little increase in the food for the villagers could be expected as the improved cultivation spread. He pointed out that back home in Wisconsin a shotgun would have solved the problem, but he had only horrified his villagers by that suggestion.

I told the Swamis that story and asked them why, when there is not enough food for everyone, they did not kill their monkeys, since in effect they killed babies and old people in order that monkeys could eat. They smiled indulgently, and replied that I ate quite a bit of wheat and rice, certainly as much as several monkeys, and I should remember that God made me, and God made the monkeys, and the babies and the old people, and who are we to decide which will be allowed to live? They took the opportunity to answer my question with a question to make clear to me their view that a human being is only a minor part of the changing scene of living plants and animals—self-conscious, yes, but not a superior being appointed to use all the rest of creation to satisfy human whims or desires.

Once, on a beautiful spring day, two of the Swamis invited me to go with them to visit a Sadhu who was established on a peak some 3,000 feet above a nearby village. He had come a few years before and had announced that he was going to live at the top of the mountain above the village. They were happy to have such a holy man living nearby, but pointed out that there was no water nor shelter there, and it was a long and difficult climb to get to the top. In spite of that, the Sadhu went up to the top of the mountain. The next day, some of the villagers climbed up with water and food and fuel, and that went on day after day. By the time we visited the Sadhu the villagers had provided a comfortable cottage, a servant, all the necessities, some dozens of books he had requested, and even kept him supplied with his favorite imported cigarettes, Navy Cut. He had a beautiful view, and no cares in the world. My first visit with a holy man on a peak in the Himalayas was disappointing as I listened to his ill-informed and arrogantly dogmatic pronouncements about the *Upanishads* and yoga, and about Mussolini as the hope for disciplined order and peace in Europe. When he told me of his master who was three hundred years old, and living in a cave in the Himalayas, I asked if I might go see him but he suggested that I had not yet made sufficient progress in my quest to be ready for such a visit. As we walked home, it was clear that the Swamis were embarrassed that we had found on a beautiful peak in the Himalayas a self-centered man who was exploiting the villagers.

In the quiet routine of the ashram in the Himalayas, when I reflected on my efforts to learn about religious ways other than my own, I realized that what started as learning about had become learning from.

That process of learning from followers of Asian religious paths continued over the years as I went back to Asia several times to gather materials that would present

Hinduism, Buddhism, and Islam from the perspectives of devout followers of those paths, and as I participated in efforts to encourage the study of Asian religions in America by helping American professors of religion study in Asia and Asian religious scholars lecture and study in' America.

As I thought about my efforts to understand religious ways quite different from mine, I realized that to make sense of their answers to my questions I would need to know a great deal more about the writings, music, art, traditions, persons, rituals, and religious disciplines they accepted as dependable religious guides. I concluded that understanding a religious way other than one's own must start with learning to see that path as it is seen by those who are committed to following it, and learning to talk about it in ways they would approve as accurate. What I was learning as I explored Asian religious paths raised many questions that seem to me to be worthy of serious consideration concerning what is true, what is good, and how a religious person might react to the given experiences of a lifetime.

What are the given realities of human existence to which we must adjust? What are the regularities of the natural environment which we must accept regardless of our preferences? Which of the given conditions of our lives can we alter or avoid? What given realities are sacred? What do you mean by ''sacred''? How is God (Sacred Reality) discovered? Is everything that happens controlled by God's will? by a divine plan? Is Sacred Reality known only as a Person, as creator and controller? How is it possible for a human to communicate with Sacred Reality (God, the Divine, the Holy)? Do the sacred realities include angels, spirits, demons, super human beings, revelations, divine judgment, rewards and punishment, heaven, hell, eternity, karma, transmigration, rebirth? or a mantra as a natural force with power over material things, thoughts, and deities? Is *ahimsa* (sometimes translated ''nonviolence'') the way possible good becomes actual in the natural world and in human affairs?

What guidance does the community offer to followers of a religious path? What is the role of group devotional practices? What is the role of ritual (for an individual or a group): as a reminder? as purification? as manipulation of individuals, or of God or Gods? What kinds of religious organizations are most helpful? What is the role of religious leaders, the priest, the members of a religious order? How can the community deal with differences in the "religious competence" of individual seekers?

How can followers of a religious path discover what is true, good, sacred? How does a seeker choose between revelations, scriptures, teachers? Must a religious seeker be empty of selfish concerns? What is accomplished by reflective meditation on religious writings, oral instructions, research, and observation of art, nature, and human conduct? Or what is accomplished by devotional meditation through worship, prayer, the arts, austerity, asceticism, ecstasy? What are the results of caring actions that are experimental tests of religious insights and of human ability to help possible good become actual? Are personal religious practices undertaken as an obligation? to gain merit? to attain salvation? to express gratitude or compassion? to become pure? to atone for actions regretted? to set a good example?

What problems persist along the way? What are the characteristics of a religious pilgrim? Does the ability to turn away from self-centeredness come through awareness of the Sacred? How can we be more sensitively aware of, and act in harmony with, what is true, good, beautiful, and Sacred in the world as known through our experience? Which of the other problems along the way may be laid aside for later consideration?

As I reflected on my experience in trying to understand religious ways other than my own I concluded that people who are committed to following different paths can live harmoniously together with mutual respect and affection when we understand our differences without insisting that our own way has an exclusive claim to truth and goodness.

The harmony among different religious ways increases when we put aside for the moment whatever divides us, when we share our understanding of the realities, beauty, and the Sacred Reality we have discovered, and when we work together to relieve suffering, increase understanding, and help possible good to become actual. That shared understanding grows when we search together for answers to the questions that arise when we are learning from religious ways other than our own.

Two

Realities In Our
Natural Environment

When followers of different religious paths observe the natural world (postponing for the moment possible transcendental interpretations), they become aware of realities in the environment that are there without regard for human preferences. They discover, for instance, that we humans find ourselves alive and conscious in a place where the sun appears and disappears regularly, giving us days, nights, and seasons that vary according to where on the earth we happen to live. All human animals here on earth have been born by the same process: from the womb of a woman, without being conscious of having chosen the time or place, or our parents, or sex, shape, color, or talents; or our inevitable aging and death.

In order to survive, we all need air to breathe, water to drink, plants or animals to eat, a relatively narrow range of temperature, and frequent opportunities to sleep. This planet where we have become conscious can provide those necessities for us. Conscious humans have been observing their environment for hundreds of generations and have been clarifying their ideas by giving names to the different realities discovered and classifying them according to a variety of perceived relationships.

In order to choose what will be accepted as true and good in following a religious way, it is necessary to know as much as possible about the regularities to which we must adjust in the complex changing realities of our natural surroundings. Such knowledge of our natural environment comes to us through our own experience and from observations made by physical, biological, and social scientists, and artists.

Physicists, when asked what we humans are given that must be accepted without choice, tell us that all animate and inanimate things observed and measured by humans are made up of complex subatomic particles forming atoms which are stable, with fixed chemical properties and a fixed electronic pattern. Atoms can combine to form stable molecules, some of which can reproduce themselves, and some cannot. All elements of our environment are subject to the force of gravity, to the force of electromagnetism, and to strong and weak nuclear forces—all this without regard for human preferences.

In the phenomena of primary concern to physicists there are regularities making it possible to repeat experiments, or to predict with considerable success the outcome of alterations in the environment. For instance, in the changing, complex, interdependent physical world we can count on heat being dissipated, energy running down, friction slowing motion, and new energy coming from the sun that appears and disappears on a predictable schedule.

All living things, including humans, have been born by a variety of complicated but regular processes, requiring a fixed time of gestation, favorable circumstances and (in most cases) the union of male and female. Living things are given reality as members of a group of individuals interbreeding within the group (humans cannot become elephants; acorns, as Aristotle noted, produce only oaks).

Where there is life there is a powerful urge to adapt ingeniously to the environment, to survive by consuming other living and inanimate things, and to reproduce as many of one's own kind as can live in the environment.

Plants, which grow in profusion on this planet, live in water and on the land in such variety of shapes and colors and sizes that they have not yet been completely classified and described by human observers. They require varying amounts of light, water, air, and nourishment which they get from inorganic sources, sometimes from other plants, and even in some cases from entrapped insects. Some live only briefly, and some for thousands of years. They alter the atmosphere and the soil and the bodies of water, and they are a source of nourishment on which all animals depend.

Biologists tell us that on this earth about a million species of animals have been classified, but there is such a variety that uncounted species have not yet been named or described by human beings. Some live only in water, some are amphibious, some live underground, some only on the surface of the land, and some fly through the air. In size they range from amoebas to insects to animals weighing tons. We human animals are given, without choice on our part, an existence entwined with billions of bacteria—living, multiplying agents—and of viruses, which are smaller than bacteria and reproduce only in living cells. The processes of life, we are told, are carried out by protein molecules, of which some twenty are essential for life, and they are controlled by DNA, a fibrous molecule carrying a specific code for its own replication and for the construction of protein molecules—and that all this proceeds without conscious effort on the part of an intelligent host.

For all living things, life can end suddenly at any time through accident or illness: death can come unsought through cyclones, hurricanes, floods, drought, earthquake, fire, poisonous plants, or by the actions of bacteria, insects, or animals (including humans). All humans, even though they escape accident or illness, will die—having declined in energy and withered quite noticeably after some sixty cycles around the sun, and very rarely will any human live long enough to see a hundred springs. Imam Ali who was a cousin and son-in-law of the Prophet Muhammad, and the first Shi'i Imam, said, "Man is a wonderful creature, he sees through layers of fat, he hears through a bone, he speaks through a lump of flesh."[2]

In the midst of this given complex of plants and animals sharing an orbiting planet, we humans find ourselves with a consciousness that seems to have been thrust upon us, capable of seeing, hearing, touching, smelling, and tasting. We are aware that we receive and recognize sense impressions, that we recall and arrange our thoughts in a variety of ways, that we observe the duration of time and relations in space. Even the ability to communicate by means of language and symbols seems to be a given that shapes our lives—in the same way that gravity is both a limiting and enabling condition of human existence. We find ourselves born at a specific place and time, in a specific nation, usually in a family, sometimes a clan or tribe, with a culture and language that bind us to a group and a way of life that shapes the way we see the world around us. We discover that we are a conscious part of a changing, complex, interdependent society of humans who live a few years with limited knowledge of our circumstances, experiencing hunger, weariness, joy, sorrow, love, acceptance and rejection. By the chance of where we happen to have been born, we are given descriptions we are expected to accept of what is real and good and possible in human existence: Hindu, Buddhist, Jain, Muslim, Shinto, Sikh, Confucian, Taoist, Jewish, Christian, Marxist, for instance.

Some of the givens that shape the possibilities open to any individual derive from past and present human efforts to manipulate nature: to produce food or clothing, to cure diseases, communicate with each other, form and govern communities, fight wars, hand down wisdom. In the air above us we are given not only sunshine and cyclones; we are given also the results of human manipulations, the noise from our mills, from planes and helicopters roaring overhead (sometimes with bombs to settle disputes). The air we breathe is scented by the trees, the earth after a rain—and by our factories, diesels, and garbage. We hear the pounding of the surf, the singing of the birds—and the sirens, the traffic noise, the music of the violin, the flute, the vina, the koto, the sitar and the gamelan. We see the mountains, deserts, seashores, and sense the texture of the stones, sand, and soil—we see buildings made of wood, mud, thatch, stone, steel, concrete, and glass.

As animals, living among all the other animals in the world, we humans have made special tools for killing each other; we kill animals for food, or pleasure, or defense, and we have domesticated or exterminated some species for our own ends. Death can come to us in many ways made possible by human manipulation: by war, traffic accident, air crash, food additives, pollution, and explosives. In our communities we face the reality of poverty and hunger in the midst of plenty, of racism and sexism, child abuse, robbery, murder, war and fear of war, of exploitation by the powerful, by political parties, dictators, democracies, religious sects and heirarchies, schools—all realities to which we must adjust, all results of human manipulation.

These "givens of civilization" will not necessarily endure for all time, nor will each individual be confronted with the same ones. But in each generation human efforts to understand and manipulate their circumstances are added to the givens of the natural world, thus creating the complex interdependent pattern of given realities to which people who live on this planet must adjust.

In Asia there are many different views of the place of humans in that complex pattern of given realities, and many different ways of using our human capacity for coping with the realities of our existence. Some Asians point out that those of us from other cultures often talk as though the natural world had been generously created for our benefit, as if human beings are at the top and all other created things are here to be used as we desire—subject only to our knowledge and skill in manipulating and exploiting the world around us. Rather, they suggest, we humans are only part of the natural world of animate and inanimate things, different but not superior; capable of causing disruptions and therefore responsible for knowing our proper place. When we act as if we were the highest form of existence in the natural world and everything else can be manipulated according to our inclinations, then we become, they tell us, the cause of the selfishness, greed, cruelty, disregard for others, and much of the destructiveness on the earth.

Followers of Asian religious paths have a variety of views about what characteristics in human nature are to be accepted as given and what human qualities can be altered. They generally share a basic wonder that humans exist as aware, conscious beings in a complex, changing natural world. As conscious animals we humans are curious, we react in different ways to our experiences, we have intentions, fears, desires, and within the limits imposed by the given realities we cannot alter we can choose how we will react to the changes in our environment. For those who see human nature in this way, the religious concern is to choose the good possibilities in the world as they can be known by conscious human beings.

The religious concern for a true understanding of the realities of human existence raises questions as to whether human nature is innately good. Are human choices naturally and spontaneously directed toward the good unless evil influences happen to prevail? Or, do individuals tend toward cruelty, violence, or indifference unless redirected by outside forces? Are obstacles to the good simply ignorance, or attachment, or self-centeredness? Is the good simply awareness and understanding, freedom from selfish desires, a compassionate caring for all the realities human consciousness can recognize?

Such speculations have been with us for a long time. In the fourth century B.C.E. the Confucian sage Mencius taught that there is little difference between human beings and animals, that ordinary people think and act much as animals do. The superior, truly human person, he said, is keenly aware of the distinction between animal and human—a distinction maintained by the human tendency to choose the good, to act in ways appropriate in the circumstances, ways that express kinship with other humans. In the third century B.C.E., Hsun Tzu disagreed with Mencius and argued that human nature, which is given by Heaven, is evil and therefore all people desire the good which they do not have, and can acquire the good only through conscious efforts.

The equally ancient *Tao-te-ching* and the writings attributed to Chuang Tzu tell us that although our inborn human nature is in harmonious accord with the changing processes of the natural world, our natural human characteristics are often warped in practice. We become self-centered as we grow self-conscious about benevolence and righteousness, and concerned with acquiring skills for bending natural things to our own selfish uses. The Way of the Tao is to resist such self-centered tendencies by acting in harmony with the continuing changes in the animate and inanimate world.

When followers of Asian religious traditions discuss human nature, they often differ as to what are the given human qualities, and as to how humans can alter their lives in the world where they find themselves. But there is general agreement that better and worse choices in how we shape our lives are distinguished by their contribution to the good that is possible in the changing circumstances of human existence. Religious choices are conscious efforts, within the limits imposed by our human nature, to act in ways that increase the harmony, the good, that can exist.

There are intriguing variations in the ways millions of men and women in many different cultures have for centuries accepted Asian religious teachings about the given realities of the natural world and how the pilgrims who follow their religious path should react to those realities.

For Muslims, in communities extending from Morocco on the Atlantic through Asia to Indonesia and the Philippines on the Pacific, the universe is created by Allah and all changes in the universe are expressions of the will of God. Human knowledge of what is true and what is good is knowledge of the divine will for all creation and for human conduct as given by revelation in the *Qur'an*. All human beings have been created with ability to receive and understand divine revelation and with freedom to think and to act. A Muslim is a person who chooses to follow the straight path of submission to the revealed will of the Creator, and knows that all human actions are subject to divine judgment.

Hindus and Buddhists say many different things about human nature, but stress that a common human characteristic is ignorance—ignorance fostered by human desires that make it difficult to distinguish between the illusory and the real. The ideal movement in the course of a lifetime is from desire and illusion to detachment and insight. The true nature of a human is recognized when a person attains enlightenment, a state of freedom from illusion that can be attained while living in this natural world.

For many Hindus, natural worlds are created in cycles by the Supreme Being, are known for a time as external reality, and then return to their source. The present universe, which will exist for some 432,000 years, is the fourth creation, and will exist in a cycle shorter and darker than its predecessors. The cyclical regularities of the natural world were established at the time of creation, and the cycles of changes for humans are governed by karma, a causal continuity extending by transmigration through many existences until the effects of all desires have been dissipated. It is an observable fact of experience that knowledge about creation, karma, and the way changes occur in the natural world has been given by revelation to Rishis, superior men capable of receiving and transmitting such information.

Buddhists have generally accepted the Buddha's teaching that humans cannot know how the natural world was created, that speculation about creation is futile. They have, however, accepted a modified form of karma as the explanation of the causal basis for changes in humans, the basis for cycles of rebirth. Central to their understanding of the realities of the natural world is their recognition of constant change, impermanence in all that exists, with the causal continuity of karma shaping everything that happens in the natural world, including thoughts, intentions, desires. Knowledge concerning what is real comes through human efforts in ways discovered by the Buddha.

Many of the Hindus, Buddhists, and Jains who share the conviction that karma controls all changes which affect a person say that changes which tend toward the good are characterized as ahimsa. Ahimsa is often translated as "nonviolence" in the sense of caring, gentle, compassionate, freeing actions increasing harmony. For many Asians, an understanding of karma and of ahimsa as given realities of human existence is necessary in order to follow a religious path, to know what is true and how humans can act in ways that are good.

Followers of classical Taoism have observed that the realities of the natural world are controlled by a process of reversion, reciprocity, return: everything changes, everything returns to its source, its starting point. Any action that goes to the extreme in one direction will be followed by action in the opposite direction. For many generations this Taoist teaching has been accepted as describing the nature of the given realities of human existence to which humans must conform or risk being destroyed. Taoists say little about how existing reality got started, but they are concerned about the regularities of the processes of change and how changes might be influenced for good. Since all changes are governed by the process of reversion, violent changes will be self-destructive by provoking equally violent responses. In Taoism, good changes that humans can accomplish in the realities of human existence come by gentle, persuasive acts that in the process of reciprocity bring about similar results. The Taoist way of reacting to the frustrations, compulsions, and violence of human existence is known as wu-wei.

Again and again, as I was trying to understand what followers of Asian religious paths believe to be given realities to which they must adjust their actions, I was told that they react to what they believe to be true about *karma*, or *ahimsa*, or *wu-wei*.

Karma, as an explanation of how we happen to find ourselves in our present circumstances, and of how we might alter them, is a significant factor in the thinking of most people in those parts of Asia where Hindu or Buddhist teachings have shaped the traditions. Those who believe in karma rarely discuss whether or not it is a given fact of existence, for they consider it obvious, even self-evident. When I ask my Asian friends to explain what they mean by karma, they often show puzzlement at such a naive question. Their concern is about how it works in detail, and how they can adapt to it. But there are common threads in their explanations, be they Hindu or Buddhist, strict traditionalists or open to modifications of their views of the natural world in the light of contemporary knowledge. They point out that when we try to understand our environment we conclude that every change has a cause, that the dependability of the world in which we find ourselves is due to the fact that the same cause (or combination of causes) will have the same effect. Karma means "action," and karma as they talk about it means that all of a person's actions derive from previous actions, and will themselves in turn have consequences—and the regularity of the appearance of those consequences can be known. Karma, we are told, is the description of how things happen when humans act.

Connections between actions may be very complex, but there is no uncaused action and no action without consequences. This means that just as there are causal relations in the physical environment (an area of lesser importance, according to some informants), there are causes and effects in our thoughts, intentions, feelings and desires. Thinking, choosing or neglecting or refusing to choose, desiring, hating, imagining, worrying, loving, being angry or indulgent or altruistic—all are acts initiating consequences for the thinking subject. Every mental action will be realized somehow in the thinker's future, unless it is modified by other thoughts or desires either immediately or belatedly. Some desires are immediately effective, while others work subtly and cumulatively, not becoming evident for a long time (in the same way that in the medical sciences doctors have discovered that the consequences of diet, of radiation, of breathing polluted air may be observable only after ten or twenty years). Each living person is made up of a complex of the effects of numerous causes that have not yet run their course.

A Swami friend explained that karma is the causal process by which our good and evil actions always get their inevitable results without any external interference, without any arbitrary judgments concerning merits or demerits, rewards or punishments. His illustration: a man whose dominant desire through his lifetime had been for sexual satisfaction might be reborn as a goat, free to roam in a herd until the desire had been exhausted, and then would be reborn in a different form shaped by other desires not yet fulfilled.

A Bhikkhu ("monk"), patiently explaining karma, said that at the billiard table, when you act by hitting the ball, it will go exactly where it was hit to go—unless you can run around the table and re-direct it with another action—even though it may not go where you intended it should. The intention, or desire, is also an act with inevitable consequences, quite apart from the consequences of the hitting. As a Buddhist, understanding karma makes the consequences of intentions a primary concern.

We are told that our present situation is the result of our previous choices, but that each moment it is possible for living, thinking human beings to make new choices within the limits of their situation, choices that can modify the results of past karma and shape the future. A human is like a boat: without intelligent guidance it is at the mercy of wind and water, but a sailor who understands the workings of wind, waves, and currents, who has the desire and takes the initiative to set the sail, can guide the boat on a chosen course within the limits imposed by the specific circumstances. It is fortunate, we are told, that we have the freedom and capacity to recognize our desires and can learn how to influence them, because desires can be dangerous. It is a truth of human existence that whatever we desire, we get, inevitably—we become what we desire. Desire itself is a real force which must run its course in the same way that other forms of energy must be directed or dissipated. Just as electrical power can be generated by the manipulatian of non-living elements, so karmic forces are generated by longing thoughts, and must be controlled because of possible destructive power.

Increasing awareness of our desires stimulates interest in the knowledge needed in order to alter the direction of our desires as wisdom dictates. Some Asian religious teachers suggest that the skills recent generations have shown in verification in the biological sciences and in subatomic physics give us hope that similar efforts will be made in observing and verifying the subtle operations of karmic forces. They say that success in such seeking is more likely to come to those for whom the separation between the human and the natural world has melted away, the misleading distinction between material and non-material, or "physical" and the "spiritual," has been forgotten, and causal relations are seen to extend throughout all human experience. For them, we humans are simply living parts of a mysterious karmic process in which we are conscious for a short time, with only a partial understanding of what is happening.

Ahimsa—commonly translated "nonviolence"—embodies insights from the Jain, Hindu, and Buddhist traditions about how to increase creative harmony in the world. Ahimsa shares with wu-wei a stress on choosing fitting reactions to the flow of surrounding circumstances and avoiding initiatives that through pursuit of selfish ends would bring harm both to the self and to others. Ahimsa is *not*-himsa. Himsa is any premeditated action causing harm, pain, or arousing passions. It is an observed fact of human existence that violent acts provoke violent reactions, that premeditated harm to others (even the intention, whether or not it is carried out) destroys oneself—so we are told by Jains, Hindus, and Buddhists. Ahimsa, as negative, came to mean not violence, not anger or arrogance or bitterness, not attachment or selfish manipulation, not inflicting suffering nor fearing suffering.

Positively, ahimsa is action in ways that are compassionate, loving, open, aware, with respect and affection and a willingness to suffer rather than inflict suffering. For the Jains, ahimsa is the basis for affection toward other humans (particularly for followers of their path, and for their religious leaders), for charity, and for reverence toward the elders and the Jinas and their traditional teachings. They teach that the practice of ahimsa guards against extremist positions, skepticism, and indiscriminate open-mindedness that would see all religious ways as leading to the same goal. It is expected that a Jain who is committed to ahimsa will be at all times diligent in the pursuit of knowledge, since true understanding is necessary in order to be able to think and act without injuring living things or their environment.

Gandhi, a Hindu who was influenced by Jain friends in his youth, said that he found ahimsa in the *Bhagavad Gita*, and accepted it as basic in his experiments with truth and his efforts to win self-government for his people. He often cited passages from the second chapter that called for courage and diligence, and liked particularly verses 56-57.

> He who is not perturbed by adversity, who does not long for happiness, who is free from attachment, fear and wrath, is called a muni of steady wisdom. He who is not attached to anything, who neither rejoices nor is vexed when he obtains good or evil—his wisdom is firmly fixed.

For Gandhi, ahimsa is a way of acting that requires constant awareness and discipline in order to avoid carelessness, indolence, apathy, selfishness, passion, or harm to others, and in order to see everyone as a friend, to lessen antagonisms and increase harmony among humans and in the natural world. For Gandhi, to follow the way of ahimsa is to act in accord with such truth as is known, without attachment to results. For him, ahimsa is a necessary pre-condition for discovering truth.

Wu-wei—variously translated ''taking no action'' or ''nonresistance'' or ''actionless activity'—is accepted by many followers of the Taoist tradition as a dependable guide for our existence in a world where reversion characterizes all that happens. Those who practice wu-wei discover choices that increase creative harmony in the world, that conform to the way things happen and also influence what happens in so far as human actions can have such influence.

The Tao does not manipulate. Harmony comes naturally in the world through reversion: aggressive, antagonistic, compulsive actions are self-defeating, for it is an observable fact that such actions provoke the opposite reactions, that force destroys itself. The stronger the force, the stronger is the resistance; the more resistance to pressures, the stronger the pressures become, even to the breaking point. Things flourish for a time, and then fade; the crooked becomes straight; anything must be empty in order to be filled. Give hatred and hatred will be returned to you, punish others and you will be punished, trust and you will be trusted. The weak overcomes the strong: water is as weak as anything we know, yet it penetrates and overcomes the hardest objects. When water is allowed to go its own way without interference, it seeks its own level, becomes tranquil, makes life possible.

The person committed to wu-wei observes and delights in the way things are, recognizes that to be alive is to be tender, yielding, and to be dead is to be stiff and hard. The follower of wu-wei sees that the empty will be filled, the full bowl will spill, that those who stand on tiptoe do not stand firm. Such a person does not harm people, does not claim credit nor display goodness, does not remember past unpleasantness or pleasure. The nonresistance of wu-wei is likened to the movement of a fish in water, or to the bending of the wise bamboo in a storm only to rise again, supple, graceful and beautiful. Those who practice wu-wei are admonished to be like a mirror, reflecting rather than trying to impress, responding and then not remembering, walking away when the action is completed, dealing with the hard while it is still easy, not competing and therefore accomplishing without negative reactions. Nonaction leads to the tranquillity that makes it possible for humans to approach the ideal of living in harmony with the world. The tranquillity that comes from wu-wei opens the way for an individual to become childlike in the best sense of the word, to be able to react unself-consciously, spontaneously, and joyously to the way things are.

Chuang Tzu, in the fourth century B.C.E., wrote about people who practiced wu-wei,

> They were upright and correct without knowing that to be so was righteous. They loved one another without knowing that to do so was benevolence. They were sincere without knowing that it was loyalty. They kept their promises without knowing that to do so was to be in good faith. They helped one another without thought of giving or receiving gifts. Thus their actions left no trace and we have no records of their affairs.[3]

As we become increasingly aware of the ways followers of Asian religious paths understand the natural world and react to it, we come to conclusions about what we think is true and good—and how we intend to act. The adaptations we achieve are myriad, suggesting a wonderful flexibility. But once a choice is made, we tend to continue with it as long as possible. Just as fish return to the streams where they were born, birds migrate on familiar routes, and mon-arch butterflies cross continents to return to their birthplace, so humans tend to prefer the language and customs of their family, the trees and hills or plains of their earliest environment, the foods they first learned to eat, and the teachings about what is true and good they heard at home. Choices that alter traditional ways of thinking and acting seem to be made reluctantly.

Yet, in contrast to this inertia, there is a streak of curiosity in us that delights in seeking always greater insight into our world. As understanding increases, we discover intriguing possibilities among the inevitable regularities beyond human control (such as the seasons), and those regularities that in fact enable new achievements (such as landing on the moon or eliminating smallpox). When curiosity is encouraged it can stimulate the free play of imagination, the creative ''what if...?'' We can move beyond merely conventional observations to exhilarating considerations of living more in harmony with the given realities of our existence.

Curiosity becomes religious curiosity when a person seeks to understand not only what is true and workable, but also what is given as good—and seeks to act in accordance with the good. For those who follow a religious path, the good is seen in the light of painful awareness of destructive forces in the natural world—forces of flood and fire, tempest and earthquake, of drought and plague. There is also the painful awareness of the continued cruelty of humans to humans, even in this century: the slaughter of millions of Jews in Germany, and of millions of men, women, and children in India and Pakistan and Cambodia; and the uncounted lives lost in other revolutions or wars of conquest or independence in Europe, Asia, Africa, and South America—many of which are now active or ready to flare in a moment. And to this history is added our awareness of the growing threat of nuclear war. There are, of course, many factors involved in the mass killing of humans by other humans, but the religious observer cannot escape a puzzled, agonizing remorse in the realization that many are victims because they are Jewish, or Muslim, or Buddhist, or Hindu, or Christian, and many are killed by devout Jews, or Muslims, or Buddhists, or Hindus, or Christians. Those who are trying to follow a religious path are also painfully aware of the great human indifference to poverty, ignorance, illness—to the way humans are often cruel, "not with the ferocity of the tiger, but with the dull insensibility of a cart wheel," in the words of Mark Rutherford.[4]

At the same time, however, we are given much goodness in the world around us. We discover that some aspects of the given are beautiful and inspiring—the clouds shifting overhead, the shape of trees and mountains, the movement of water in lakes and streams and oceans, and the play of light and wind over all; the colorful variety of birds and their songs, and the graceful play of animals; the harmonies of form, color and texture in paintings, sculpture, and buildings; the harmonies of word and thought in poetry and prose, and of tones and tempos in music; and the generous consideration one person shows to another, the love within a family and loyalty to a community, the help given freely after a catastrophe. It is good that we can know at least something of the reality that is given, and it is good that we may alter some aspects of our environment and ourselves.

To a religious person, the good is a given that is found beyond the individual, that exceeds any individual's personal preferences or desires. Certain ways that things happen can be recognized as inherently better than others. In any circumstance, the better ways may be difficult indeed to ascertain, but the method of discovery, like that of the sciences, involves sensitive and careful outgoing curiosity and observation. Such a posture of committed outgoing entails a certain diminution of self, as the person seeks to move in accord with what appears to be good, rather than pursuing limited personal goals. This is why the study of karma suggests working for detachment from personal passions; and why ahimsa requires compassionate concern for all the given realities we perceive; and why wu-wei calls for the best activity possible in each situation, quite apart from what seems to be personal advantage. In religious seeking, self-concern and self-assertion increasingly yield to growing wonder and awareness of the world, which in turn yield to the forces of truth, beauty, and goodness that are found in our environment.

During a lifetime in the natural world here on our planet, human reactions to the perceived realities of the natural world play an important role in determining what is seen to be true and good. We react to reality as we see it in myriad ways: with despair, fear, or sorrow, with resignation, shame, or bitterness; other times with trust, hope, curiosity, or with joy, playfulness, or laughter. Some react by simply adopting the habits and traditions of the social group into which they were born; some react with a self-centered concern for their own comfort and happiness; some submit to what they think is their fate. My observations have brought me to the conclusion that the person who reacts with awe, and then acts spontaneously as the way opens in the light of awe and wonder, can be said to have started on a religious path.

Up to this point, I have limited these comments to the given realities of the natural world as described by persons who claim to know it through their senses, usually avoiding what followers of Asian religious paths say about reality they recognize as divine or sacred. Of course, this is an artificial separation, for one of the givens of human experience is that all around us are religious groups insisting that their rituals and teachings about the divine are the means by which truth and goodness are known. But when I recall the Asians I have known well and admired for their religious insight, it seems to me that the quality of their religious life includes a spontaneous reaction of wonder and awe and gratitude before the beauty, complexity, regularity, goodness, and joy they find in the world around them—in spite of the obvious suffering and cruelty and stupidity and indifference in human society. I found that only after recognizing their reactions of awe could I progress in understanding their religious practices, what they teach, and what they trust. The traditional religious teachings they had accepted from their communities seemed to me to be worthy of serious consideration when I was told about them by a person who had a sense of having been in the presence of Reality that is Sacred.

Awe starts with the discovery that in the complex, interdependent, changing, mysterious, puzzling world as it is given to humans, many of the regular changes are understandable, many can be influenced by humans. Awe and wonder grow with repeated discoveries—in spite of cruelty and misfortune—that some events are good, even amazingly good, and some are beautiful, even breathtakingly beautiful, and sometimes there are moments of joy.

Awe, rising from those discoveries, leads to an awareness of a force at the heart of the changing world that is kindly, patient, yielding, generous, may even be called loving, merciful, and compassionate—a persistent movement toward harmony, toward what human observers may call the good, a tendency that can prevail, that makes good life possible. That force, movement, tendency, process (whatever it may be called, and however it may be described as tender, loving, compassionate, caring) is seen with awe as holy. For those people whose wonder grows out of such awareness, the religious path is a way of life conforming to, and expressing reverence and gratitude to a Reality seen as Sacred.

Three

Realities Seen as Sacred

Followers of religious paths tell us that in addition to what can be understood about the natural world through painstaking observation, manipulation, and analysis, they have had glimpses of aspects of reality greater than humans can manipulate or fully understand. They say they have become aware of reality seen with awe as good, as caring, compassionate, making possible the good found in the natural world. As observers of the natural world and human reactions to it, they discover that spontaneous awe and gratitude open the way to awareness of the sacred.

What name should be used for reality that is a mystery sensed with awe and reverence? Any name that pleases. Up to now, no universally acceptable name has been found, nor does it seem urgent that it should be. In my tradition, I am content to call it God. Here, it is often called Sacred Reality simply to avoid using any of the familiar names that are attached to specific traditions.

Some followers of Asian religious ways say that if you know God you do not talk about God: that attempts to talk about such a Sacred Reality or to prove or disprove the existence of such a reality by skillful rational demonstration are "like scooping the moon from the water," in the words of the Patriarch in *The Journey to the West*.[5] They say that theological and philosophical speculations are necessary and significant, but are more effective in protecting us from inconsistencies, incoherences, and emotional excesses than in introducing us to new discoveries about religious realities in the world around us. Sometimes it is suggested that words by themselves, however skillfully used, can only hint at the sacred, that they need the help of insights expressed by music and other arts, and of the beauties of the natural world, and of caring, compassionate actions in human society.

Back in the 1930s, at the University of Michigan, when Bertrand Russell was relaxing after his lecture on *The Existence and Nature of God*, he remarked that he had intended to start on a light note with a story, but when he saw the intent faces of the students he decided it would not be fitting. The story he omitted was of what happened to him in the first world war when he was arrested in Britain because of his pacifist opposition to the war. As he was being questioned, his jailer asked, "What is your religion?" When he replied, "Atheist," the jailer looked up in surprise and asked him to spell it, then looked at the puzzling new word for a moment, smiled and said, "That's a new one. But we all believe in the same God, don't we?" At the time, I wished Bertrand Russell had told the story so the students would have that question in mind as he talked about the existence and nature of God. I remembered the jailer's assumption many times in Asia—when a Hindu said that all paths lead to God; when a Muslim said that there is only one path to God; or when a Buddhist said there are many paths leading to many deities, but there is no path leading to One God.

When I ask my Asian friends about Sacred Reality, their answers have often introduced me to new insights, shown me the need to re-examine many of my own ideas, and moved me to take seriously the differences in religious insights held by people who are admired for their integrity and devotion to truth. I have dismissed with little effort the wearisome repetition of traditional formulas and generalizations memorized and recited automatically; and have dismissed without serious consideration the arrogant claims to know a God of vengeance who is a protector or manipulator of a particular clan, or caste, or nation, or geographical area, or traditional culture; and have listened with embarrassed reservations to claims to know all about God's will, or a divine plan for individuals and for nations. The answers to questions about Sacred Reality bring new insights and encourage self-examination when they come from men and women who have a sense of awe and reverence in their view of our world, who have been open to new discoveries, have been compassionate and loving toward their fellow creatures, and whose choices are made in an effort to live in harmony with what they know of Sacred Reality. The diversity in their answers suggests that while awareness of the sacred is widespread, it is seen in many quite different ways.

Sacred Reality is impersonal for many followers of the Hindu tradition. *The Brihadaranyaka Upanishad* tells us that, "There was Brahman at the beginning..." and this Brahman was characterized by *neti, neti*, "for beyond saying 'not this, not this,' there is nothing else possible."[6] Some Hindus say that Brahman is pure consciousness and therefore all that at first seems real to individual human beings is illusion, that only the ultimate, the unchanging, the one can be real. Some Hindus say that religious understanding starts with the recognition that there is a Supreme Being worthy of reverence, a Being so great that all efforts to describe divine attributes are useless speculation. Others see Brahman as the cause of all that exists, a transcendent creative force that can be described by such impersonal terms as Infinite, Eternal, Absolute, One, Highest, Independent, Supreme. Brahman, they say, has the powers of creation, preservation, and dissolution of the world; and in the continuing relations of all that has been created, the divine purpose is revealed. Brahman is absolutely true, good, and blissful—and thus truth, goodness, and bliss are qualities of all that has been created. Brahman is the unchanging source of beauty in the world.

According to some of the earliest Buddhist traditions, the Buddha taught that it is the wrong question to ask if there is a Sacred Reality back of all that exists, that it is meaningless to ask if there is One God, a creator and controller of the world, for such knowledge is unattainable by humans. Later, one of the distinctive points of difference between Mahayana and Theravada Buddhism was that Mahayana taught the Triple Body of the Buddha. The Earthly Body of the Buddha (Nirmanakaya) is known as the Buddha Sakyamuni of India, as Bodhisattvas, and as present in images and other visible forms. The second Body of the Buddha, the Subtle Body (Sambhogakaya), manifests Buddha-wisdom through an unbroken continuity between the supreme third Body and the truths of human experience; it contains all Buddhas and is known only through the meditations of the most highly developed Bodhisattvas. The highest Body of the Buddha is an impersonal reality, the Unmanifested Body, known as the Body of the Dharma (Dharmakaya), an indescribable positive reality, beyond the dualism of the one and the many, beyond causality, beyond subject-object thought, beyond change and decay, beyond selfhood, desire, bliss. The Unmanifested Body may be spoken of as void, or emptiness, but both terms are inadequate and misleading in English except as they suggest the impossibility of assigning attributes or powers to the awesome Dharmakaya. "Not this, not this" seems to be appropriate when talking about the Buddha Body of the Dharma for it is incomprehensible when viewed from the perspective of the causal patterns known through the observation of physical objects.

The discovery that the awesome, impersonal void can be known through human experience led some Mahayana Buddhists to the conclusion that compassion is a characteristic of reality. Ours is a benevolent world where, in spite of ignorance and attachments, humans can through acts of compassion attain the Buddha wisdom that frees them from further involvement in suffering and constant change. Brahman for some Hindus, and the Body of the Dharma for some Buddhists, have been for many followers of those religious paths the Sacred Reality that is revered is impersonal, free from limitations, and benevolent.

For followers of classical Taoist thought as found in the *Tao-te-ching*, the revered impersonal reality is the *Tao*:

> There was something undifferentiated and yet complete, which existed before heaven and earth. . . . I do not know its name; I call it Tao. . . . The Tao that can be told of is not the eternal Tao; the name that can be named is not the eternal name. . . . Tao is hidden and nameless. . . . The thing that is called Tao is eluding and vague. . . . We look at it and do not see it. . . . We listen to it and do not hear it. . . . We touch it and do not find it. . . . Tao is empty (like a bowl). It may be used but its capacity is never exhausted. . . . The Great Tao flows everywhere. . . . It accomplishes its task, but does not claim credit for it. . . . Yet it is Tao alone that skillfully provides for all and brings them to perfection. . . . It becomes one with the dusty world. . . . Deep and still it appears to exist forever.[7]

Tao has been translated into English as: way, course, method, order, norm, moral order, physical order, right conduct, unchanging and underlying unity, impetus to live and to move, principle, reason, providence, heaven, God, logos, Supreme Being. *The Tao-te-ching* presents the Tao as a mystery beyond comprehension. It is not defined, it is only given a label. For those persons whose religious perspective has been influenced by the *Tao-te-ching*, the Tao is an acceptable label for the impersonal reality that is revered as sacred. Chuang-tzu has this to say about the Tao:

As for the Way, it is something with identity, something to trust in, but does nothing, has no shape. It can be handed down but not taken as one's own, can be grasped but not seen. Itself the trunk, itself the root, since before there was a heaven and an earth inherently from of old it is what it was. It hallows ghosts and hallows God, engenders heaven, engenders earth; it is farther than the utmost pole but is not reckoned high, it is under the six-way-oriented but is not reckoned deep, it was born before heaven and earth but is not reckoned long-lasting, it is elder to the most ancient but is not reckoned old.[8]

In other Chinese religious teachings, as gleaned from the writings of Confucius, Mencius, Hsun Tzu, and Mo Tzu, the revered impersonal reality is often referred to as *T'ien*, usually translated into English as "Heaven" (which can mislead unless the sense in which "Heaven" is being used is clearly defined, because both words have many different connotations in their respective languages). Hsun Tzu (d. 235 B.C.E.) wrote:

The fixed stars make their round; the sun and moon alternately shine; the four seasons come in succession; the Yin and Yang go through their great mutations; the wind and rain widely affect things; the ten thousand things acquire their germinating principle, and are brought into existence; each gets its nourishment and develops to its completed state. We do not see the cause of these occurrences, but we do see their effects—this is what is meant by the influence of the spirits. The results of all these changes are known, but we do not know the invisible source—this is what is meant by the work of Heaven. Only the Sage does not seek to know Heaven.[9]

Heaven may be thought of as an ethical principle that is shaping all reality, making it possible for the good to exist; again, Heaven may be another name for nature, for all that exists with its puzzling complexity and changing aspects. Heaven is seen as an impersonal force requiring no external guidance or control, a power to which all living beings must conform in order to live. In that sense, Heaven may be thought of as destiny, or may be the name for everything that humans cannot control. Heaven is often spoken of with awe and reverence as a mystery ultimately beyond human comprehension. Hsun Tzu, in the passage quoted, wrote, ''therefore if a person neglects what men can do and seeks for what Heaven does, he fails to understand the nature of things.'' The Sage, a person who has attained the highest possible levels of knowledge and virtue, does not try to know Heaven, the ''invisible source'' of all the changes humans perceive.

Brahman, the Cosmic Unmanifested Buddha, Tao, T'ien—these are different ways of expressing trust in an impersonal Reality recognized with reverence and awe, such awe that words are adequate for little more than giving a label. There are other Asian ways of describing impersonal Reality, but these four illustrate widely held views. For many Asians the impersonal Reality is a mystery so great that, although they dare to assert that it is, they are unable to describe with equal confidence the details of what it is other than to say that they find it a dependable source of such compassion and harmony as can be known in human experience. Others tell us it is possible to discover some of the ways the mysterious impersonal Reality shapes the world, possible to know some of the characteristics of Sacred Reality through observing the natural world and human experience, through fleeting glimpses of a Reality that might be missed by observers who do not know how or where to look.

The glimpses might come through the words of a teacher, or from mind-stretching writings, or from the arts. We may glimpse Sacred Reality in the marvels of the natural world: in the regular turning of the seasons and the interplay of growth and decay all about us, or in the complex coherence extending from the microscopic to the vastness of outer space, discovered through mathematics and the sciences. We can also have glimpses of sacred reality in worship, and when we see generous and trusting human relations, or watch the unself-conscious play of a child. The belief that those fleeting glimpses are of a Reality underlying the variety of human experience comes to those humans whose awareness gives rise to wonder which may become reverence for some aspects of experience seen as sacred. That impersonal Sacred Reality remains mysterious, never fully known, difficult to describe, but for many followers of Asian religious paths it is as real as the air they breathe, the light they see, the sounds they hear, the water that nourishes all growing things.

For many other religious people in Asia Sacred Reality is perceived as a Divine Person who is the creator, sustainer, and controller of everything. As a Person, God's will, purpose, goodness and beauty can be revealed to humans, and humans can know that their creator is a Divine Person who is caring, judging, forgiving, compassionate, loving, merciful, patient, just.

Among the Hindus I have known, I cannot recall one whose trust in a sacred reality was limited to Brahman as an impersonal being about which nothing could be said. Often, when asked about Brahman, they would mention the neti, neti admonition and then say that they "leave Brahman to the pandits"—and would shift to talking about "God in action" as Shiva, Kali, Vishnu, and the like. Vishnu, for example, is Brahman known as Vishnu, who created this world and has taken various forms at different times when it was necessary to restore righteousness on the earth. Vishnu as cosmic creator is commonly depicted sleeping on the sea of milk, with the sacred lotus issuing from his navel. Well-known stories of his particular embodiments have him active in the world as, among other things, a boar, a dwarf, and a man-lion. Kali, Shiva's consort, is the divine creator, sustainer, and destroyer in female form— the Holy Mother who gives us birth, nourishes us at her bosom, raises us up, and wrings our necks (for the same power that creates us always destroys us). Shiva, in the form of the Dancing Natarajan, creates and sustains the earth in a joyful dance.

Some of us who have tried to understand Hinduism starting as outsiders, be it from an Islamic or Judaic or Christian or Buddhist or secular background, have been intrigued by hearing a Hindu's devout and enthusiastic description of Shiva's creative activity as *lila*, as play, as sheer fun: spontaneous, surprising, joyful activity without necessity, or any desires, or needs for satisfaction. This divine play of a Personal Deity, as presented in the beautiful image of the Dancing Natarajan, is offered as a true description of how reality was created in the beginning and how creation continues. Seeing the creative activity of a Personal God as lila, as God dancing in the playful joy of creating, avoids claims to know what God was thinking while creating the world, what results God expects, and how God controls the natural world and humanity.

The stories associated with the image of the Dancing Natarajan suggest the possibility that lila motivates the reality that surrounds us, that joyful spontaneity might be an important ingredient of a religious way of reacting to the world we humans perceive. After puzzling over what my Hindu friends said about lila, I found that when I observed religious arts, the natural world, and human relations in families and caring communities, I discovered not only new insights and a sense of wonder, but often a sense of joy. My awareness of spontaneous joy and hope in the world has increased through having my attention drawn to beautiful Indian bronze images of the Dancing Natarajan, images telling us how some Hindus see Sacred Reality as a God with personal characteristics.

Islam, unlike Hinduism, offers no distinction between an impersonal God and a personal God—there is only one, Allah, with all the divine qualities as revealed in the *Qur'an* where the 99 names of Allah include: All-forgiving, All-compassionate, All-hearing, All-seeing, Allmighty, All-powerful, All-gentle, All-merciful, Allpreserving, All-knowing, All-wise. The fervor of Muslim concentration on the traits of the Divine Person is embodied in the wide-spread practice of ritual repetition of the names of God (dhikr). Such recitation or "recollection" underlies a good life for a follower of the straight path of Islam who is thus constantly made aware of Allah as creator and sustainer of the world.

   Once, in Cairo, when I spent an afternoon with half a dozen Islamic teachers who were patiently answering my questions, I asked them which of the Islamic writers my students should read when they were being introduced to the study of Islam. After a lengthy consideration of the possibilities, they agreed that the students should first study the *Qur'an* and then might read al-Ghazali (who died in 1111 C.E.). After Muhammad, no one Muslim speaks for all followers of Islam throughout the world, and al-Ghazali is not universally accepted as an authority, but most Muslims, Sunni or Shi'i, would agree with what he says about God in his *The Revivification of Religion*:

> God is One, the Ancient of Days, without prior, Eternal, having no beginning, Everlasting, having no end, continuing for evermore. . . . He is the First and the Last, the transcendent and the immanent, Whose wisdom extendeth over all. . . . He cannot be likened to anything else that exists nor is anything like unto Him, nor is He contained by the earth or the heavens, for He is exalted far above the earth and the dust thereof. . . . He is the exalted, Almighty, puissant, Supreme, Who slumbereth not nor sleepeth: neither mortality nor death have dominion over Him. His is the power and the kingdom and the glory and the majesty and to Him belongs creation and the rule over what He has created: He alone is the Giver of life, He is Omniscient, for His knowledge encompasseth all things, from the deepest depths of the earth to the highest heights of the heavens. Not the smallest atom in the earth or the heavens, but is known unto Him, yea, He is aware of how the ants creep upon the hard rock in the darkness of the night: He perceives the movement of the mote in the ether. He beholds the thoughts which pass through the minds of men, and the range of their fancies and the secrets of their hearts, by His knowledge, which was aforetime. All that is other than

Him—men and jinns, angels and Satan, the heavens and the earth, animate beings, plants, inorganic matter, substance and accident, what is intelligible and what is sensible—all were created by His power out of non-existence. He brought them into being, when as yet they had no being, for from eternity He alone existed and there was no other with him.[10]

The creating and sustaining nearness of Allah is known through the Qur'an and through the writings of admired Islamic scholars, and is experienced daily by ordinary Muslims as they observe the natural world around them: the alternation of night and day, the rain sent down from heaven to revive the earth, the clouds driven by the winds between heaven and earth—surely those are signs for people who have understanding. The intimate ties between Allah and his creation are beautifully illustrated in a story told to Annemarie Schimmel by a friend in Turkey:

> The sheikh of the Khalvati order in Istanbul, Sunbul Efendi, in looking for a successor, sent his disciples forth to get flowers to adorn the convent. All of them returned with large bunches of flowers; only one of them—Merkez Efendi—came back with a small, withered plant. When asked why he did not bring anything worthy of his master, he answered: ''I found all the flowers busy recollecting the Lord—how could I interrupt this constant prayer of theirs? I looked, and lo, one flower had finished its recollection. That one I brought.'' It was he who became the successor of Sunbul Efendi, and one of the cemeteries along the Byzantine wall of Istanbul still bears his name.[11]

In Islam, Allah is recollected as a mysterious Being, the Creative Power, Guardian, Bestower, Aware, beyond human comprehension, beyond human description, One, before Whom all Muslims bow in submission, willingly, in wonder, in awe, and in gratitude.

Many followers of different Asian religious paths are quite clear that God is a Person who creates the universe with plan and purpose, and whose will is shown in everything that happens. All regularity, all that can be known, manifests the divine intention. For them, God is a judge enforcing the divine order with penalties or rewards, and dispensing grace in mysterious ways. There are some hundreds of millions of followers of Asian religious traditions who see reality as God's creation, who believe they know something of God's will, and who expect to be rewarded or punished for their conduct.

But many other devout followers of Asian religious paths find that what they have experienced as awe-inspiring Sacred Reality is too limited when it is described as a person, or as the manifestation of divine creative will. These pilgrims question whether a good life—a wise, caring, generous life—depends on the acceptance of speculations concerning where the world came from, why it came into being, and what purpose the whole world is seeking to accomplish. They try to avoid the conflicts between followers of religious paths who claim to know God's will, how God thinks, what God likes and dislikes—as if humans could know and even anticipate the inner workings of a Divine Mind—whether those claims are based on revelations transmitted for centuries, or on insights received recently by persons specially favored by God.

There are also many Asians for whom the Sacred Reality includes superhuman beings, embodiments of sacred powers, whose functions are more limited than universal creation and control. Such beings include many Hindu Gods and Avataras, Shinto Kami, and Buddhas, Arahants and Bodhisattvas.

Hindus tell us that the Supreme Power is apparent in our human world in myriad ways. That if you think you can count the Gods and begin with the three, Brahma, Vishnu, and Shiva, you will discover there are thirty-three, three hundred and thirty-three, three thousand three hundred and thirty-three, that the Divine takes many forms. The creator Gods have often taken a particular human form (as an Avatara) for a special purpose—as when Krishna came as an Avatara of Vishnu to bring harmony to the world, or Rama came to set the example of a just ruler, and Sita his wife as an example of the ideal of womanhood. Durga is the Divine Mother. Lakshmi is the Goddess associated with good fortune in business. Saraswati is the Goddess of learning, the helper of the student. Ganesha, the God with the elephant-head, is the patron of innovation, bringing good fortune when called upon at the start of a journey, of a dance, or of building construction. Hanuman, the monkey God, is the model of loyalty, a hero in the Ramayana epic and transformed in China to the celestial monkey, Wu-k'ung, carrying out the wishes of the Bodhisattvas in the heavens.

In Japan, the followers of Shinto find themselves in a world pervaded by Kami, which are whatever is worthy of reverence in the world. Such Kami are not only encountered in human forms but may be the Kami of clouds, wind, sun, moon, stars, animals—each having its own function to perform and all working harmoniously together moving and controlling everything that exists. The highest of the Kami is Ama-terasu-o-mikami, the Sun Goddess, endowed with the virtue of the sun's rays and embodying the harmonious unity of the Plain of the High Heaven, the upper world. The Sun Goddess consults with other Kami, helps them and calls on them for help. Motoori Norinaga (1730-1801) wrote of Her:

> We must bear in mind that there is no line which divides heaven and earth, and that the Plain of High Heaven is situated above all countries. And since the Sun Goddess rules heaven and illuminates every corner of heaven and earth, thus without her blessing no country on earth can exist even for a single day or single hour. In short, she is the most precious Kami in this world.[12]

Most Mahayana Buddhists agree that there have been many Buddhas; that the Buddha known as Gotama or as Sakyamuni is the great Buddha of our era; and that the Buddha Maitreya is yet to come. As recorded in the sutras,

Sakyamuni Buddha lived on the earth as a human who attained enlightenment, and continues now as a superhuman being in the indescrible state of Nirvana. Any Buddha is a superhuman being worthy of respect and gratitude.

Bodhisattvas are beings who, having attained freedom from attachment or resistance to any aspect of natural or supernatural reality, have compassionately vowed to put off becoming a Buddha in order to continue to help all suffering beings attain Nirvana. Free from ignorance or selfishness, a Bodhisattva lives with love and compassion in harmony with all natural forces. The Bodhisattvas have distinct traits or personalities, and work in different ways to relieve the sufferings of the world. Manjusri, for example, is the embodiment of wisdom for cutting through the clouds of ignorance. Samantabhadra brings karuna, loving mercy to guide humans to freedom from attachment or resistance in the experiences of daily life. Maitreya, cherished and honored under many names throughout the Buddhist world as the Buddha yet to come, is the Bodhisattva who is making it possible to recognize that benevolence is an inherent characteristic of our world.

Reflection on the personal traits of the Bodhisattvas can offer reminders and insights into the nature of the religious path. For example, Avalokitesvara, the Bodhisattva of compassion, is presented at Angkor in great images having faces looking in the four directions, and in the Kathmandu valley by enormous eyes painted on the four sides of the tower rising over the temple—symbolizing the universality of compassion for all suffering beings on earth. Avalokitesvara was originally represented as a male figure, but in China and Japan, the same Bodhisattva is widely revered in female form as Kuan-yin in China, and Kannon in Japan. When I asked Buddhist friends how contemporary Buddhists explain the great popularity of this female personification, they said that there is, of course, the delightful old story of the Chinese girl, Kuan-yin, who compassionately gave her eyes to her blind father but that is only a story. They said that since we so often see compassion expressed by women, it is fitting to represent it in a feminine form. But, ultimately, they urged, when you realize that there is no difference between Avalokitesvara and Kuanyin, that Kuan-yin is Avalokitesvara, you see more clearly that compassion is neither a male virtue nor a female virtue, but a characteristic of any person following the Path. They suggested that it is not fitting to use either "she" or "he" when talking about any Bodhisattva.

Buddhists who accept the Buddha's teaching that the human mind is incapable of knowing a universal creator say there is no supreme being controlling all human affairs. However, many Buddhists, while remaining skeptical of the possibility of knowledge about a supreme Creator-God, accept without question the reality of many Gods. Often these are Gods from Hindu traditions, or from other traditions widely known in their own part of the world; sometimes such Gods are depicted as having been converted to Buddhism by renowned teachers (as we are told happened when Mahinda brought Buddhism to Sri Lanka).

These Gods are generally seen as having superhuman powers only at the level of the desires and perils of ordinary daily life—of health, prosperity, and good fortune—with no power in the most important aspect of human existence, the attaining of enlightenment. The Buddhists I have known who would talk about Gods seemed to regard them as they did their government leaders and functionaries, as beings with considerable power who might be malevolent or benevolent and must be manipulated, placated, cajoled, and on occasion obeyed, but were not objects of devotion.

A complete list of supernatural beings considered to play a significant role in human affairs might include jinn, nats, phis, nagas, ghosts, angels, and other local spirits—I have not had enough experience of them to be able to make any significant comments, and so have turned my attention to other aspects of the religious ways found in

Asia that seemed to me to be more important.

Reality, according to most Asian religious teachings, includes levels of existence in addition to the earth as we know it: places where God, or Gods, or superhuman beings dwell, and where humans may exist after their life on the earth. The names given to those real places are often translated into English as "heavens" or "hells," but those words can be used only with the warning that their usual connotations may be misleading. Followers of Asian religious paths have usually, with unquestioning confidence, included heaven in their descriptions of the real world; often, but not always, they have also described hells where the inevitable consequences of evil actions or indifference are punished or atoned and the demands of justice are met.

Among Hindus we hear of seven worlds down and seven worlds up, with descriptions of beings inhabiting them for varying lengths of time. They are places where Gods dwell, where a jiva (an individual embodied self) exists and may be rewarded or punished between transmigrations. Hindus and others who have accepted karma as an accurate description of how changes occur in reality find that heaven and hell, all realms other than the earth, are also under karma.

In Mahayana and Tantric Buddhism there are many Buddhist Lands: the lower worlds, such as the one where the God Yama judges by reading the book recording the actions of those who come there; the world of hungry ghosts; the animal world; this world of human beings, of suffering, of limitations, often called the world of patience and endurance; the world of fighting demons, such as the world where the celestial monkey Wu-k'ung performs his heroics in *The Journey to the West*, under the guidance of the Bodhisattvas; the Tushita Heaven, still in the realm of desires from which the Bodhisattvas come to this human world; and the higher worlds, the Buddha Lands, such as Amida's Land of Bliss and Purity where those who correctly call upon the Name and Thought of the Buddha (in Japan, the Nembutsu: *Namu Amida Butsu*) can attain rebirth in a realm in which it is possible to attain enlightenment.

In Islam, the reality of heaven and hell has been revealed in the *Qur'an*. It is a fundamental belief of Islam that after death every mortal must face a Day of Judgment from which those who have been judged worthy will be sent to Heaven, a paradise where all possible good and beauty can be enjoyed. Those individuals who have been judged to have broken God's commands will be punished in hell.

The reality of these various supernatural places is established, we are told, by divine revelations, and by superior humans whose teachings about reality have been accepted as trustworthy. Those revelations and insights tell us there must be places where evil acts are punished and good acts are rewarded. Although generally accepted as realities, some pilgrims along the way have questioned what they were told about heaven and hell. Among Muslims, especially among Sufis, Rabi'a (in the second century after Muhammad) is remembered for having prayed, "Oh God, if I worship Thee for fear of Hell, burn me in Hell, and if I worship Thee in hope of Paradise, exclude me from Paradise; but if I worship thee for Thy own sake, grudge me not Thy everlasting beauty."[13] In an oft-repeated anecdote, when Rabi'a was asked why she was running down the road with a torch in one hand and a pitcher of water in the other, she replied, "I am going to light a fire in Paradise and pour water on to Hell, so that both veils may completely disappear from the pilgrims, and their purpose may be sure, and the servants of God may see Him, without any object of hope or motive of fear."[14] Although her reservations are remembered, they have not been widely shared.

Questions about the existence or nature of heavens and hells are raised among followers of other Asian religious paths, but usually not pressed because discussion of such issues upsets their fellow pilgrims. For instance, many years ago I asked a distinguished Burmese Bhikkhu, an able scholar admired as a devout Buddhist, to write an article about basic beliefs of Theravada Buddists. When I received the manuscript I took it back to him and pointed out that he had not said anything about the planes of existence—and that a leading Buddhist layman of his country had recently lectured at Columbia University in New York City on the thirty-one planes of existence as basic to any understanding of Buddhism and of how humans can cope with the world as it is. My friend explained that he had not treated the planes of existence because if he said what he believed to be true the more conservative of his Buddhist compatriots would be terribly upset, and the more modern and liberal of his Buddhist colleagues would take him to task—and it would distract all of them from the truly important things he wanted to say about Buddhism. In the end he included a brief paragraph about the thirty-one planes of existence and then turned to issues he considered much more important for understanding reality: the chain of causation and the attainment of Nibbana.

After asking religious leaders from many different traditions what they hold to be true and good about the realities they see as sacred, I find it impossible to make general statements about what is sacred that would be acceptable to all of them. Their answers describe sacred realities as known in the natural world just as all other realities are known; or as transcendent yet also appearing and recognized in the natural world; or as only transcendent, known through divine revelation. They speak of Sacred Reality as an impersonal Divine Process, or as a personal Divine Being, or as many different personal Divine Beings. They tell us of supernatural beings dwelling in supernatural places, and of humans who have had supernatural powers. Their answers vary widely in the importance attached to the realities described. What they say about realities seen as sacred becomes clearer when they discuss the ways humans can adjust to, and live in harmony with, sacred realities.

As I wandered around in Asia with many opportunities to ask sincerely religious men and women what they hold to be true and good, I was selecting some of their answers as worthy of serious consideration, and putting others aside (perhaps because I did not understand them). The answers I found most instructive came from people who recognize that the truths they accept about the given realities of the natural world are extended by given sacred realities which open up possibilities for good that otherwise would not be realized. For them, there are realities which are not good (such as accidents, illness, ignorance), which set limits on human actions, are destructive, and to be avoided if possible. And for them there are also realities that are good, setting limits and opening up possibilities for benevolent creative human actions. For many of them, realities seen as good are sacred.

From such a religious perspective, each of us has been born into a world where we are involved in given natural and sacred realities in the midst of which some human awareness and some good actions are possible. In addition to what has been said above about Asian answers to questions about human nature as observed in the realities of the natural world, we need to consider what they tell us about how our given nature as individuals is involved in sacred realities.

Involvement in the realities of the natural world comes, we are told, through each individual's initiative in gathering sense impressions and reasoning about them, guided by memory and cooperation with others in communities of like-minded people. Religious seekers who see sacred Reality as a personal creator and controller tell us that an individual's involvement with the sacred realities of daily life comes about through divine initiative and revelation. Those seekers who see Sacred Reality as impersonal tend to say that such involvement in the sacred comes through insights gained by individual initiative using skills developed in communities of seekers over many years.

Whether individuals become aware of the sacred through revelation or human insight, their interpretations of the sacred are usually made in communities of followers of religious paths. They tend to participate in communities of seekers who are convinced that some knowledge of Sacred Reality is possible, and that such knowledge gives individuals guidance in their adjustment to the realities of their lives.

Most followers of Asian religious paths believe that Sacred Reality (personal or impersonal) controls the givens of our world that make each of us responsible for our desires and actions. They tell us that when our choices have been in harmony with the given Sacred Realities of human existence, the consequences will be good; and when they have not been in harmony, the results will be evil, may even be terrifying. The consequences of human choices and actions—whether made certain by God, or Gods, or Brahman, or Bodhisattvas, or Sunyata, or karma, or T'ien, or the Tao—are predicted in a variety of ways: they may come to fulfillment in this lifetime, or may determine for each of us the nature of our continuation after death. The given reality that continues after the death of the body is described as a soul, or spirit, or jiva, or Atman, or karmic consequences of desires from previous existences in the natural world.

Orthodox Muslims believe that every person has a soul. Once, when I asked a Muslim scholar, an internationally respected member of the Ulama (leaders recognized as rightly-guided teachers whose interpretations of Islam can be trusted), how he knows that there is a soul, he replied that there can be no doubt as to the reality of souls because the truth about them has been revealed in the *Qur'an*. On the basis of his careful study of all Qur'anic references to the soul and of many commentaries on those passages, he said that the soul remains a mystery; it is not described in the *Qur'an*; the soul is the source of vitality in each individual, and when it departs the remainder is lifeless; it is a supernatural reality incomprehensible by human minds; it survives after the death of the body and will be present at the Day of Judgment.

For many Hindus, the continuity of transmigrations from existence to existence in the natural world is caused by human desires and ignorance about the true nature of the Atman. Little more can be said about Atman than that it is, and that to see Atman as separate from Brahman is an illusion. The true awareness that Atman is Brahman clears up the illusion of the reality of the separateness of an individual self, and ends the cycles of transmigration. In its individual form as temporarily embodied in living things, Atman may be known as jiva and recognized as an aspect of the divine that has become known in partial and often distorted ways. The jiva carries the moral consequences of its actions in previous existences, and is thus the channel for the causal continuity of karma in all living beings. My Hindu friends point out that when Atman is translated as "soul" it may be misunderstood since there are several connotations of Atman in different schools of Hinduism, and a variety of interpretations of soul in Judaism, Christianity, and Islam.

For Hindus, transmigration explains how the unbreakable causal continuity of karma makes it inevitable that each individual will receive the good and bad consequences of all actions, thoughts, and desires. For that to happen, there must be continuation of life from one existence to another. Through the Rishis it has been revealed that the Atman is a permanent Self which transmigrates from existence to existence in embodiments shaped by the consequences of previous lives until all consequences for past thoughts and actions have been fulfilled and no new causal actions, thoughts, desires, fears, or hopes have occurred, and the Self then realizes its indentity with the Ultimate Brahman.

Once when I was visiting a Hindu temple with a Swami friend, I saw a beggar whose swollen legs and open sores were so terrible that I stopped and gave him a coin. He cursed me, and threw the coin away, and the Swami explained his reaction to me. The beggar had seen that I gave the coin out of pity, and he would accept no such condescension. He knew that his present circumstances obviously resulted from wrong-doing and ignorance in a previous existence, and that he must let the bad karma work itself out without adding to it by rebellion against his illness or by persistence in the evils of that former life. Rather than risk additional unfavorable karma by trying to support himself, he chose to sit in his suffering at the temple and receive alms; but he did not have to endure pity because he was suffering for past actions. The Swami hinted that such an indignant reaction to an obvious fault in another person might create more bad karma for the beggar—at the same time that my condescension created bad karma for me.

To help me understand the inevitability of transmigration, the Swami told the familiar story of the Hindu sannyasi who, after many transmigrations, had in this existence become free of all desires and would not be born again. As he lay on his bed waiting for death he looked out the window and saw a deer with a broken leg—and his spontaneous compassion for the suffering animal was enough of a binding attachment to make him be reborn once more in a life just long enough to exhaust that last desire.

The Buddha taught that there is no soul or self or Atman or jiva. An individual is simply an aggregate of distinguishable parts, an aggregate formed by the consequences of actions in previous existence. At death those parts disintegrate, leaving only the karmic tendencies acquired in this existence, which then shape the form of a new aggregate, a new person who will be born. Some Mahayana sects say the Buddha taught that all humans are born with the Buddha-nature and will eventually become Buddhas.

Buddhists speak of rebirth rather than transmigration

because the Buddha taught there is no Atman nor jiva to carry the karmic consequences from birth to birth. The difference between the Hindu and Buddhist teachings about the continuity of karmic consequences from birth to birth was explained to me at Nalanda by Bhikkhu Kashyap (d. 1976). He grew up in India as a Hindu, and later became a distinguished Theravada Buddhist scholar whose life exemplified unself-consciously those qualities of compassionate awareness sought by followers of the Theravada path. The Buddha, he said was a radical reformer of Hinduism who rejected the *Vedas* as a revelation from a God or Gods, or even as inspired scriptures. The Buddha rejected talk about deities, and the belief that anything could be known by humans about creation or a creator—all we could say about creation would be useless speculations by conscious creatures about what was before there was any consciousness. The Buddha rejected the religious rituals of the Hindus as simply useless external forms, and rejected their austerities as self-indulgence, often undertaken for the impression they might make on others. He rejected caste distinctions. He rejected the Hindu belief in Atman as speculation for which no proof is possible. But the Buddha accepted karma as a given reality which is as obviously a condition of human existence as sunshine, or wind, or water, or fire.

The Buddhists have retained rebirth as an inevitable implication of the continuity of karmic processes (which they sometimes call "the chain of causation," or "dependent origination," or "interdependent causation"). Since there is no Atman (no self or soul, no jiva—no entity of any kind to transmigrate from one existence to another, or to be judged, punished, or rewarded), then what is reborn can only be the consequences themselves of the previous existence. In the mysterious process, vitality is transmitted, and the conditions for individual human lives are set, growing out of what has happened in previous existences. Once when I was questioning a deservedly distinguished

Japanese Buddhist scholar about the differences between Buddhist sects in Mahayana and the extent to which he perceived common elements with Theravada Buddhism, he said that in all Buddhism as he knows it the common bond is an acceptance of the principle of dependent origination, of the continuation of effects from a previous existence.

Buddhists simply consider the chain of causation a true description of how life takes place in this world: our desires, past and present, for external things and internal satisfactions cause us to experience round after round of birth, sorrow, lamentation, pain, grief, despair, old age, death, and rebirth. Sometimes these experiences are misunderstood as rewards and punishments, or as just judgments by external powers—when in fact they are the result of ignorance of the nature of human existence. Fortunately, it is possible for human consciousness to awaken to a Reality beyond the transient causal chain of ordinary human experiences, a Reality beyond ordinary description, named in various ways as Nirvana, Satori, Other Power, Sunyata. The awakened consciousness of that Reality brings freedom from the cycle of rebirths.

The process of individual involvement in the sacred realities of human experience is referred to by Hindus, Buddhists, and Jains as *dharma*. The word has been used in different traditions with such a variety of meanings that anyone talking about dharma should make clear the sense in which it is used. A common, and unsatisfactory, translation of dharma into English is "duty." Early in my stay in Hindu ashrams I was surprised when, having thanked a Swami for a kindly favor, he replied casually, "Oh, it is only my duty." It did not seem to me that he had acted as if he were fulfilling an inescapable obligation to a bewildered guest, and I did not understand until I discovered he had been taught that "duty" is the English word for "dharma." He had thought he was saying that he is not to be thanked or praised for simply doing what comes naturally, what is obviously fitting in the circumstances, what is the natural outcome of the combination of karmic forces in which the two of us found ourselves. "Oh, you shouldn't mention it. I was simply following my dharma."

Dharma sometimes refers to the revelations received from the Rishis and transmitted through the Vedas, or to commentaries on those revelations. It may refer to the teachings of the Buddha or to Buddhist doctrines. Dharma is often translated into English as "law," carrying the meaning of natural law, or civil, criminal, moral, or religious law. Sometimes it is used in the sense of virtue, or righteousness, or a moral code, or religious ideals, or of correct practice in following the path that leads inevitably to the good and the true, to *moksha* (release from transmigration or rebirth), or to Nirvana (freedom from all binding attachments, from all frustrations, disappointments, pain, ignorance, desires). Dharma is associated with the belief in karma, and transmigration and rebirth, the belief that what we desire we will inevitably get, that what we think and desire, as well as what we do, shapes what we become. Dharma is the process in which individuals involved in the changing realities of human existence choose better or worse and take the consequences.

In several of the religious traditions of Asia people think of themselves as living under the watchful eyes of recording spirits or deities who, from above the earth, note every specific merit and demerit of their thoughts and actions, thus determining the nature of their future existence in another realm. The demerits are subtracted from the merits, and a balance of merits results in of some form of blessing either on earth or in a higher realm after death. When there are more demerits than merits, the appropriate punishment will be a less desirable life on earth or in a hell. Sometimes it is believed that superior beings—Buddhas or Bodhisattvas, for example—have acquired an excess of merits far beyond their own need and may dispense that store to persons who, for one reason or another, receive special consideration.

The Muslim follower of the Straight Path starts with belief in the Day of Judgment, one of the fundamental beliefs of Islam. On that Last Day, the Day of Resurrection, Allah judges each person on the basis of the choices made during a lifetime on the earth, and awards eternal blessings in paradise to those whose actions were in accord with the divine purpose as revealed in the *Qur'an*. Eternal punishments will be the lot of those who have been indifferent or antagonistic, for God is just. For a devout Muslim, the Day of Judgment is a basic reality of human existence.

Imam Ali, the first Shi'i Imam, tells in his Eighty-sixth Sermon the significance of the Day of Judgment for the follower of the Straight Path of Islam:

> The creation of human beings is a proof of His Might and power; they did not come into existence of their own will and desire; their births, their growths and their mental developments are all subject to the laws of creation as decreed by Him; they are (physically) bound to obey them. As in their births, so in their deaths they have no choice and no power. At the time of their deaths their souls are withdrawn from their bodies, and the bodies are thrown into graves where they disintegrate. Then, each one of them will be resurrected individually, and will be rewarded according to his deeds. During their lifetime, they had all been given chances to achieve their emancipation and salvation; they had also been shown the correct ways to attain them; and were also given time and opportunities to reach the realm of His Grace and pleasure. They had been provided with fair and normal chances to dispel their distrusts, misgivings, perplexities and doubts about religion. Then, they were given complete liberty in this world of thoughts and deeds to think as they like and do as they desire so that they may train their minds and with the help of such trained minds, free will and the span of life allotted to them, they may find the purpose for which they were created. The lifetime vouchsafed them was enough to attain eternal blessings and to provide for hereafter.[15]

But the Sufi, Khwaja 'Abdullah Ansari (d. 1089 c.e.),

doubted that the Divine Judgment was simple adding and
subtracting:

> O God,
> You made creation gratis
> You provided sustenance gratis.
> Have mercy on us gratis:
> You are God, not a merchant!

> O God,
> What cares he for Heaven who is searching for you?[16]

The followers of Asian religious paths describe in
quite different ways the consequences of human involvement in realities seen as sacred (such as heaven, hell,
reward, punishment, transmigration, rebirth), but they
generally agree that the given realities of human experience extend beyond what is ordinarily thought of as the
limits of the natural world; and that something of the reality seen as sacred can be known; and that, whether known
as a Process or an Impersonal Power or a Person, the Sacred
Reality shapes human actions. The Sacred remains a mysterious Reality, a Reality not altogether separate from the
world we know through our senses and our reasoning, yet
known in an awesome way that is more than we can en-
compass by our own efforts. When we are confronted by
glimpses of realities more sublime than we have imagined,
we discover that we forget ourselves as we become involved
in realities experienced as sacred. That forgetting of selfish
concerns frees us to live more harmoniously in the given
circumstances of human existence.

Individuals who choose to follow a religious path find
that along the way there are many quite different communities of seekers whose insights often provide helpful guides
toward ways to live more harmoniously with the given natural and sacred realities that set the limits for human life.

Four

Guidance Some Asian Religious Communities Offer

When I considered what followers of Asian religious paths said is true, and good, and sacred, and how their insights are to be expressed in actions, I became increasingly aware that the initial guidance for following a religious path comes from the community into which we are born, instilling a perspective that is usually preferred throughout a lifetime. The close-woven texture of religious community life—be it Sikh, Shi'i, Tibetan Buddhist, Confucian, Hindu, or whatever—varies in detail from place to place and tradition to tradition, but is everywhere accepted as a given reality confronting each individual who is born there. Community religious guidance comes through scriptures, persons who are honored and trusted, rituals, arts, and acts of unself-conscious compassion.

Questions arise for those persons who, after starting to follow the religious path of their community, discover that there are many different scriptures, religious insights and revelations, honored leaders, revered rituals, inspiring arts, and ways of expressing religious insights in action. How do they choose the guidance they can trust?

In Madras in the 1950s, I had a long discussion with a Brahman friend about my plans to edit a book written by Hindu scholars to present their religious ways from their own point of view rather than as seen by an outsider. His concern lest I should naively be led astray moved him to write this letter:

You know the Harvard University's publications, in the Harvard Oriental Series. We refer to the admirable and scholarly edition of Vikrama's Adventures, forming Volume 26 of that series. This is an exact quotation from page 248 (the words in brackets are the editor's explanation and not translation of the original): "As they were thus conversing agreeably with pleasant questions, at that time, somewhere, a certain Gauli [the more usual Gauri, name of Civa's Consort] cried out with a loud voice. Then the king askt him: 'What does the Gauli say?' and he answered: 'The Gauli says that in the north-flowing river a corpse is approaching, in water up to the navel.' A moment later, in another place a certain Civa [Gauli] cried out; and being again askt by the king the man said: 'A great loin-cloth containing ten thousand gold coins is coming down [the river], tied about the hips of that same corpse.' The story goes on to say that both the predictions turned out true and the king was delighted by the cleverness of the man, with the usual consequences of such delight, etc."

Now, please have a clear picture of the story as thus narrated and then add up this information that we give. The word *Gauli* has two other meanings, one a wall-lizard and the other, a female fox. These meanings are apparently not known to the Sanskrit scholars of Bombay and Bengal, as they are not found in Sanskrit dictionaries published there, but are well-known here in South India (Dr. Raghavan would verify this). Here, many millions of people believe that when the wall-lizard taps on the wall, the lizard speaks, prophesies, and a really learned man is expected to be able to decode at once those sounds. And most of the annual almanacs here go on publishing the key, i.e., on such and such a day of the week, the tapping in such and such a direction foretells such a thing. Those millions of people would deem it irreligious or at least defying fate to do anything or to continue anything which is contra-indicated by the lizard.

Just as millions of people believe this, many millions of people have never looked into these almanacs and do not know that people believe in this portent. At any rate, none of the scholars who took part in the Harvard University publication was aware that the whole point of the story is gone, which was to show, not that the God Shiva's consort appeared and said something, but that the lizard spoke and to show what an accomplished man that hero was and how he succeeded in life. (Similarly, the female fox's cry heard in the adjacent woods conveys its meaning to those who know.)

The points we wish to illustrate are: (1) India is so vast and its colonisation and history have been so different for its really innumerable parts that constitute this continent, that nobody knows even any such general common features as would authorize him to say, "Let me explain this aspect of *India*." He can talk about some portion of Bengal, or of Guzerat, but not of India. (2) When we (Indians) do travel outside our own insignificantly narrow world, either bodily or in books, we feel that we are *foreigners* venturing into new worlds. When we read books about India, its religion or marriage customs or eating habits, written by Indian foreigners or "foreign" foreigners (it does not make the slightest difference) we are simply amazed. We can quote other illustrations from other books of similar highest repute, but we have either explained our point already, or we have no point to explain.

Hinduism in India is not one religion, but hundreds. At any place it is a compromise between what the Aryas brought there and what they already found there and in what century this happened. The details of the faith as known in Tanjore District are not what they are in Tennevelly or in Godavari District (all in this one Province). Inside one district itself, they are not the same as known to and believed in by the Brahmin master, his Brahmin servant and the master's non-Brahmin friend. For one man or a dozen men to purport to write of Hinduism is not merely to get a result which would be wrong in almost all its details, but would be conveying an altogether wrong idea of the complex nature of Hinduism itself. The only persons who would be satisfied would be the writers (who know that they are in the right and all who differ are in the wrong) and perhaps some of his readers inside his own Province.

Many times since, when I have tried to say what seems to me to be true about an Asian religious path, I have imagined my Brahman friend looking over my shoulder, skeptically.

Scriptures may be revered writings seen as the words of the Supreme Divine Being recorded and transmitted exactly as revealed, or may be cherished writings accepted as authoritative elaborations of truths presented by persons who have received revelations or have had inspired insights. Some followers of Asian paths hold that a religious way must begin with divine revelation, that religious insights can only come to individuals chosen to receive them. Others teach that religious insights have come to persons who have developed the characteristics needed in order to perceive sacred realities.

Millions of Hindus have traditionally held it to be true that the Supreme Being revealed "that which rules authoritatively over mankind" to the Rishis, the first human sages, who preserved "that which is heard" in the form of the *Vedas*. For many centuries, the pupils of the Rishis recited the revelations to their pupils, preserving the accuracy of the text down to the last syllable by checking their words with a recited mnemonic key. Only in more recent times have the Sanskrit words of the *Vedas* been passed from generation to generation in written form. The prayers, hymns, and sacred instructions of the four *Vedas* are the supreme authority, but most Hindus have been more influenced by the scriptures known as *Smriti* "that which is remembered," such as the *Ramayana*, and *Mahabharata*, and the sectarian scriptures, sacred romances, codes of laws, and manuals of philosophy.

For millions of Muslims it is true that the *Qur'an* was revealed by God to the Prophet Muhammad, dictated to him in Arabic over a period of twenty-three years, immediately recited by him to his followers, written down in its revealed form under Uthman, the third Caliph, and preserved without variation since then. The *Qur'an* reveals the relation between God and the world, the true nature of the world, and the path of virtue for humanity. "And We reveal the Scripture unto thee as an exposition of all things, and a guidance and a mercy and good tidings for those who have surrendered (to Allah).''[17]

The followers of Shinto see the Sun Goddess, Ama-terasu-o-mikami, as the Supreme Deity ruling everything in the heavens and on the earth—like the sun, giving and maintaining life everywhere and governing all change with the help of the Kami. Motoori Norinaga (1730-1801 c.e.) is enthusiastically thankful that he was born in Japan, the land of the original revelation:

> Unfortunately, foreign countries, which have lost the ancient accounts of the divine age, have no way of knowing that the Sun Goddess is to be venerated, and they reduce, based on the speculation of human knowledge, the movements of sun and moon to the activities of yin and yang. In China, the Heavenly Deity is regarded as the most precious, supreme being, whereas in other countries some other deities are venerated. But such deities were concocted by mere speculations and given certain names, but what is known as the heavenly Deity or the Way of heaven has no reality. It is lamentable that foreign countries venerate such beings who are unreal, not knowing the Sun Goddess, while we must be grateful to know the legacy of the Sun Goddess, thanks to the ancient legends of the divine age which have been correctly transmitted. Indeed, our country, being literally the homeland where the Sun Goddess was born, is destined to be the great center of all other nations.[18]

Since the power of the Sun Goddess has been revealed, and the legendary accounts of that revelation have been correctly transmitted, it can now be known in detail by human insights. It can be recognized, we are told, by anyone who has contemplated a pine tree against the sky, or wondered at the playful antics of young animals, or watched the eruption of a volcano. The sacred, they tell us, is recognized by humans in the natural world because it has been revealed by the Sun Goddess.

Most Buddhists do not conceive their scriptures as revelations given to humans by a Deity. But in Mahayana Buddhism, some of the writings are accepted as revelations from Bodhisattvas. Nichiren, in Japan, found the *Sutra of the Lotus of the Wonderful Truth* to be such a sacred revelation that even to recite its name with full devotion would bring an ordinary person to enlightenment. Some Tantrics, Hindu or Buddhist, claim to have received revelations as a result of the compulsive power of their austere practices.

Those who have accepted their chosen revelation as unique, or as replacing all other revelations, have a firm basis for rejecting all other revelations offered as guidance for following their religious path. Those seekers who find it difficult to choose between revelations or have not yet become aware of any revelation, find that they must evaluate the contents of revelations just as they do the other forms of guidance found in the different communities of followers of religious paths.

Much guidance has come from writings cherished as the religious insights of humans, known and unknown, who had remarkable talents for discovering sacred realities. These may be preserved as holy, or may be accepted simply as embodying unusually enlightening and inspiring thoughts. Sometimes they derive special authority from the person who wrote them, or who is treated in them. Sometimes the authority rests on insights accepted as penetrating, even when little or nothing is known about the writer. Some of these guides are offered by religious institutions, while others maintain their popularity among large numbers of individuals without being sponsored by any organized group.

Muhammad's acts, or comments made on his own initiative (that is to say, not under direct revelation or dictation), were recorded as Hadith, and his judgments serve as a trustworthy guide for followers of the Straight Path. After the revelations of the *Qur'an*, there are to be no more prophets, no more direct revelations; but there are Sufis and religious leaders who are recognized as rightly-guided— superior persons with such understanding as does not come to ordinary people. And for the Shi'is there was Ali, whose perceptions are preserved in his writings, and there were the other Imams, either seven or twelve, revered for their wisdom. Instructions received from Muhammad, or Ali, or from Sufis or Imams or Shaikhs, or Mullahs judged to be inspired, can be as binding as the commands of the *Qur'an.*

Jains follow the writings of the Jinas, persons who attained superhuman powers, became omniscient, and provide the most noble examples that can be known; the sacred writings of the twenty-four Jinas have been preserved in the *Angas,* cherished as the highest truths made known to humans during the last 2,500 years. The all-knowing, enlightened teacher, the Jina of our era is Mahavira, who died in India in 527 B.C.E. He is venerated as a man who was raised to divine status by following disciplines that freed him from desires and brought him to omniscience. The guidance of a Jina concerning what is true and what is good is the guidance of a man who has attained knowledge of all reality, natural and sacred.

The Sikhs (the name means "disciples") are followers of Guru Nanak, who died in 1539 C.E. after forty years as a teacher working in the Punjab to establish a new pattern of religious belief and daily life that would unite Hindus and Muslims in one community. His teachings are preserved in the *Guru Granth,* which includes a collection of the hymns of the Gurus who followed Guru Nanak in the sixteenth to eighteenth centuries, and also selections chosen by the Sikh Gurus from writings by Hindus and Muslims from the twelfth to seventeenth centuries. It brings together the sacred writings of superior persons in a form designed to be used in ritual worship and to provide guidance for conduct.

The Buddha, after many previous existences, was born in the sixth century B.C.E. as a prince in the Sakya tribe. In that existence he attained enlightenment and for several decades taught what he had discovered. His teachings, about natural and sacred realities and about how others might also attain enlightenment, have been preserved through the centuries, chiefly in Pali, Sanskrit, Chinese, Tibetan, and Japanese, together with sectarian commentaries in many languages. For Theravada Buddhists, the *Tipitaka*, the Three Baskets of Discipline, of Discourses, and of Ultimate Things, present the true teachings of the Buddha. The *Dhammapada*, in the Second Basket, and the Jataka Tales of previous existences of the Buddha, are popular guides to conduct which overcomes the barriers of lust, hatred, superstition, and delusion that hinder followers of the Noble Eightfold Path of Buddhism.

Mahayana Buddhists receive guidance from many Sutras telling of the teachings and actions of many Buddhas. One of the most popular is the one chosen by Nichiren as supreme, the *Sutra of the Lotus of the Wonderful Truth*, inspiring followers of the Path with its awesome stories of the teachings and powers of the Buddhas and Bodhisattvas. For some, it is so powerful that simply to recite its name with devotion gives the guidance needed for following the Path; for others, chanting the Lotus Sutra is a purifying act. In each case, the Sutra is the means by which humans can reach out toward the Sacred. Tibetans focus their study on the *Kangyur* (the Buddha's teachings translated from Sanskrit originals, plus four Tantras) and the *Tangyur* (revered writings by Buddhist scholars). In China and Japan, where many of the early Buddhist writings have been translated and discussed for centuries, followers of the Buddha have usually been associated with schools that grew up around writers of widely accepted commentaries on the Sutras: such schools as T'ien-t'ai, the Pure Land of Amitabha, and Ch'an (in Japan: Tendai, Shin and Jodo, and Zen).

In Chinese tradition, the *Tao-te-ching* has been treasured by many religious seekers even when they belong to no specific group or institution that accepts it as a scripture, or uses it in religious rituals, or regards particular Taoist persons as sources of sacred authority. Also in China, for many centuries the *Analects* of Confucius have had the status of revered writings, trusted in the family and the nation as giving powerful insights into reality and good conduct, often quoted in the Master's words. Among the Chinese seekers of the true and the good, innumerable followers have found either the Confucian or the Taoist view to be the most insightful known.

The guidance received from sacred writings is enhanced by commentaries written by men and women who have sought human understanding of the true and the good through reflection on the scriptures. Examples of traditional commentaries would be the writings of al-Ghazali in Islam; of Shankara or Ramanuja in Hinduism; of Buddhaghosa, or Nagarjuna, or Shinran, or Tzongkhapa in Buddhism; of Mencius or Chuang Tzu in China. In every generation religious leaders, theologians, and philosophers continue adding to the vast literature of commentaries. More recently historians, critics, linguists, sociologists, and psychologists have added their assessments, using a variety of developing resources and skills.

The different Asian religious traditions are united in believing that humans are given opportunities to know something of the sacred—either through direct revelation, or through insights attained by superior individuals. Each tradition preserves with reverence the writings found most revealing and sustaining. To each new individual, these texts are offered as containing the best guidance for life, accumulated over many generations. Thus these writings have played an important role in shaping the lives of millions of our contemporaries.

The follower of a religious path who studies the sacred writings cherished by devotees of different religious groups faces some difficult questions. How can one be sure that a scripture has been revealed by a Sacred Being? How can anyone choose between different revealed scriptures? Whether sacred writings have been traditionally accepted or only recently brought forth, how does a religious seeker know if the insights are true?

Guidance for following a religious way also comes from person to person. Some religious communities say that understanding of the sacred and motivation to religious actions can come only through loyalty to a person, that sacred writings and rituals and arts and devotional practices are only reminders of the awareness of the sacred that has come from a person who has inspired us to follow a religious path. That person may be remembered from the past as a religious leader with special qualifications for guiding an individual to clearer awareness of the sacred, or may be a contemporary teacher, friend, or parent. Commitment to a religious path, we are told, almost always comes through trust in an admired person whose insights are accepted as true.

The remembered person may be regarded as the founder of a religious path, such as Muhammad, or Sakyamuni Buddha, or Mahavira, or Guru Nanak, or as an inspired interpreter and follower of a chosen path. A Shi'i remembers Ali, or the other Imams; a Sunni may have been inspired by Rumi, or al-Ghazali, or Ibn Arabi—and both of them may cherish certain Sufis. There are Buddhists who have been guided by Nagarjuna, or Rinzai, or Dogen, or Tzongkhapa, or Shinran. There are Hindus whose path has been outlined by Rishis, or Shankara or Ramanuja, or more recently by Ramakrishna or Ramana Maharshi. Guidance from parents or friends or teachers or leaders in a religious group determines for many followers how much attention will be given to religious concerns and which religious path, if any, will be followed: "my father used to say," "my mother taught me," "the priest said," "my teacher opened my eyes to," "the Bhikkhu was the kind of person who," "our Mullah taught," "when we asked the Dalai Lama, he said," "the Swami told us," "when the Shaikh decided that." For a great many followers of Asian religious paths, what they believe about our human condition is based on what they believe some revered person said or did.

The contemporary leaders of religious groups (usually male, but that is changing) are sometimes chosen on the basis of birth: as reincarnations in Tibetan Buddhism, or as sons of priests in some Hindu and Buddhist traditions. Sometimes they are chosen from volunteers who have been trained in the traditions of the group as in Islam, or in the Buddhist Sangha. Usually, the leaders are recognized with ceremonies confirming their special powers and the followers of religious paths hold their rightly-guided and properly designated leaders in high regard: their Priests, Swamis, Bhikkhus, Shaikhs, Imams, Tulkus. The persons recognized by the community as religious leaders may teach, may be concerned with the health and welfare of their followers, or may perform the ceremonies and rituals required by the religious traditions of the group.

Chuang Tzu, in the 4th century B.C.E., suggested a possible reason for trusting the guidance of a superior person in his story about the man who had suffered the public disgrace, as was the custom in China at the time, of having his foot chopped off for a crime. He said,

> Plenty of people who have whole feet laugh at me because I haven't; I get into a furious temper, but if I go to the Master's place the mood has passed before I come home. I do not know whether it is the Master cleansing me by his goodness or my own self-awakening. I have been going around with the Master for nineteen years now, and was never aware that I'm a man with a chopped foot.[19]

Such a superior person as Chuang Tzu's Master who inspires spontaneous forgetting of oneself would have at least some of the qualities needed for guiding followers of a religious path, whether or not authority to guide had been conferred by public ceremonies, or the cleansing power of his goodness had been recognized by the community.

It is obvious that religious teachings about what is true and good are transmitted in sacred writings and pass from person to person, but I find it remarkable that religious ideas are so frequently personified. Sacred Reality is presented as a Person who has a will, who judges, punishes, rewards, who may be angry or sad or pleased, may be influenced by human petitions and offerings. Dependable truths about Sacred Reality (however named), and about realities seen as sacred, come through persons recognized as authoritative, trustworthy, inspired, and therefore to be revered. Sometimes we are told that they are supernatural persons such as angels, or spirits, or Bodhisattvas, or Gods, or Kami. Or, the revered transmitter may be a superior human such as Muhammad, or Ali, or Sakyamuni Buddha, or Confucius—or a less well-known, but still authoritative person of unusual insight such as the founder of a local sect, or a monk or nun, or a teacher, or a parent; or the Master of the man with the chopped foot.

When religious perceptions are cherished in indissoluble association with a revered person through whom religious insights have come, any questioning of those insights may be taken as an affront, as a challenge to the authority of a person who is honored and loved. When religious ideas are presented as true because of the person who taught them, personal loyalties can be barriers between the followers of different paths. Decisions as to which teachers are "rightly-guided" have often caused bitter divisions between followers who are loyal to different persons, quite apart from questions concerning the truth or falsity of their teachings.

Even though loyalty to a person seen as rightly-guided may be divisive, may be misleading, or may be used as a means of manipulating followers of a religious path, many people have initially been attracted to a religious way by a person they admire, and have remained followers because of their loyalty to a person. Such identification of a person as a model and an authority for what is true and good is a means often used by religious communities to attract followers to the religious guidance they offer.

The problem of choosing which person to follow, of evaluating conflicting claims to authority, is not a new one. The Theravada Buddhists remember the conversation of the Buddha and the Kalamas, from over twenty-five hundred years ago:

> The Kalamas said, "venerable Sir, many religious teachers
> come to our place from time to time and expound their respec-
> tive doctrines in detail. All of them say that what they preach
> is the only truth and the others are wrong. Thus, while glorify-
> ing themselves and their doctrines they find fault and despise
> others. Now, Sir, we are at a loss. How are we to know which
> of these teachers speak the truth and which speak falsely?"
> "Yes, Kalamas," said the Buddha, "it is quite natural to
> doubt where doubting is proper. Now come, do not accept a
> thing merely because it has been handed down by tradition or
> from generation to generation or from hearsay. Do not accept
> a thing because of mere scriptural sanction, nor by mere logic
> or inference, nor by superficial knowledge, nor yet because of
> your fondness for some theory, nor because it seems to be suit-
> able, nor again just out of respect for a certain religious teacher.
> But, Kalamas, when you know for yourself that certain things
> are unprofitable, blameworthy, censured by the wise, and
> when performed or undertaken conduce to loss and suffering,
> then you should reject them."[20]

My own biases, centuries later, are exposed when I make a positive summary of the negative advice to the Kalamas: Yes, twentieth century Kalamas, it is always appropriate to ask questions. Use logic, critically-examined theories, and devotion to evaluate cherished scriptures and traditions, and to discover what action is fitting in the circumstances. Show respect for any teachers who have helped you in your inquiries. In the end, you who are seeking must decide for yourselves what leads to clearer understanding, to harmony, to the good—and then you should follow that path.

Followers of a religious path, in their common search for the true and the good, normally participate in rituals that express their commitments and aspirations. Through such rituals, they seek a clearer sense of the Sacred, reaffirm their convictions, and encourage and guide their fellow seekers. The effectiveness of rituals and ceremonies lies in their conformity to familiar patterns and in repetition, whether performed by a gathering in unison or repeated alone in private. In performing ritual acts an individual may express wonder and gratitute and aspirations, may seek reminders of the religious truths ceremonially symbolized, may reaffirm convictions held, may seek clearer awareness, and may act in ways that benefit other members of the community.

Community ritual worship takes many forms. Participants in religious rituals may be reminded of the religious traditions of their community through ceremonies designed to inspire them and reaffirm their commitments. The ritual may be commemoration of a person, an event, or a scripture as interpreted by a recognized leader, or by the arts through images, paintings, instrumental and choral music, or architecture. They may be ceremonies of seeking for clearer understanding and for consistency in following a religious path. Rituals may be repetition of carefully formulated private or public prayers of veneration, supplication, gratitude, aspiration, awe. The ritual may include acts of preparation, such as posture, clothing, diet, pilgrimage, study—and acts of consequence such as efforts to share whatever one has, to relieve suffering, to reconcile conflicts, to enlighten, to promote harmony.

Most rituals are firmly located in time: daily, weekly or fortnightly, at times set by the movements of moon or sun or stars, or by the dates of special events in the traditions of their community. Daily, for example, Muslims are expected to pray at five set times. Hindus should greet the dawn each day by reciting the Gayatri mantra, ''We meditate upon that adorable effulgence of the Resplendent Vivifier, Savitar; may He stimulate our intellects,'' thus recognizing their dependence on the orderly appearance of the sun and helping to maintain harmony on the earth. And Sikhs are enjoined daily to recite this morning prayer written by Guru Nanak:

There is one God,
Eternal Truth is His name;
Maker of all things,
Fearing nothing and at enmity with nothing,
Timeless is His Image;
Not begotten, being of His own Being:
By the Grace of the Guru, made known to men.
As He was in the beginning: the Truth,
So throughout the ages,
He ever has been: the Truth,
So even now He is Truth immanent,
So for ever and ever He shall be Truth Eternal.[21]

In the Buddhist Sangha, and in many different Mahayana Buddhist sects, the day begins and ends with meditation following traditional methods taught by their leaders.

Throughout Asia, major religious festivals are ritual occasions for remembering, celebrating, atoning, and affirming—in a variety of ways. In India, for example, Diwali is the festival of lights celebrated throughout the country with many different interpretations of its significance. At the time of an eclipse, in India, millions of Hindus will be bathing in rivers, lakes, or the ocean, knowing that they have joined in a common ritual act at the same time. Ramadan, in Islam, is the month of fasting, a time of atoning and forgiving, of training in patience, an expression of thankfulness for divine blessings. In Theravada Buddhist communities, Wesak, which comes at full-moon time in May, is the great festival commemorating the birth, Enlightenment, and passing into Nirvana of the Buddha. Through major religious festivals the followers of religious paths gain a strong sense of a religious community from their realization that the same ritual actions are being performed by hordes of other people who share their commitment to what they believe to be true and good. They get much the same sense of belonging to a wider community through participation in the Muslim pilgrimage to Makkah, or the Hindu pilgrimage to Varanasi, or the Buddhist pilgrimage to Bodhgaya.

Some of the most popular Asian religious ceremonies are those in which the community celebrates the sacred mysteries of suffering and joy in the events of family or individual life—birth, coming of age, marriage, and death. The times and places for these rituals are, of course, set by the circumstances, as are the rites associated with pilgrimages to sacred shrines such as those at Badarinath, Sarnath, Amritsar, Najaf, Fes, Lhasa, Tiantai, Kyoto and Ise.

Since religious ceremonies embody fundamental beliefs of a community, the details of practice receive minute attention. For example, ritual posture for worshipers is an important consideration because the position and movements of the body influence the mind, and when many people assume the same posture and perform the same gestures together, they are more closely bound into a community. In a mosque at the daily prayers, when lines of devout Muslims repeat together the same prayers, and in unison stand, bow, kneel, touch their heads to the floor, then stand again—it is a moving experience, whether shared with a few others, or several hundred, or even thousands at large mosques on major holidays. Muslims are reminded daily that throughout the world the ritual of daily prayers is being repeated by millions. In Buddhist or Hindu temples, the posture may be the lotus posture, or kneeling; circumambulation of the image or shrines proceeds clockwise, since presenting the right side expresses respect. The movement of the hands, and the way they are held during worship, has special significance also in some traditions. Ritual postures and bodily movements are recommended as conditions that make worship more effective.

Details of clothing also play a role in religious culture and ceremonies. In some parts of India, Hindu women are expected to have their heads covered, in other parts not. Among Muslims there is wide diversity in the regulations governing how women shall be dressed when they come to the mosque, or even walk through the streets: in some countries it is decreed that women be veiled and clothed to their ankles, while in others women are free to choose the clothes they will wear in public. In all the religious groups of Asia the recognized religious leaders wear special costumes for performing religious rituals, and sometimes for street wear to identify their special status. A Swami may wear an ochre-colored robe. A Theravada Bhikkhu's robe may be made of many pieces of yellow cloth sewed together symbolizing the early robes made of rags found in rubbish heaps at Varanasi when the Buddha founded the Sangha; and the Bhikku may wear it with one shoulder bare, either the left or the right according to the preference of the sect. The Tibetan monk may have a deep red robe, and his particular sect can be recognized by the color and shape of his hat. These random examples only hint at the variety of clothes traditionally identified as proper on various Asian religious paths.

Traditional group worship may take place where the architecture and environment have been designed to encourage devotional communication with Sacred Reality. Often specific consecration must precede the effective ceremonial use of a temple, shrine, or image and continuing purity of the place is a primary concern of some devout Asians. For some, the purity of a sacred place can be lost through the presence of a person who comes from another religious culture. Although there are signs of change in recent years, Hindus have generally held that the place of worship must be properly purified and that the presence of non-Hindus or members of the lowest caste would make the place unsuitable for worship until it had been ritually reconsecrated. In Iran, and at the Shi'i shrines in Najaf and Karbala, even the special pleas of Shi'i friends could not gain me admission to the mosques. In Morocco a law forbidding non-Muslims to enter the mosques—passed under the French colonial rule to avoid the strife caused when ignorant and thoughtless European tourists wandered into the mosques—is still in effect. In Istanbul I saw European tourists walk in a mosque wearing shoes and taking flash photographs of the men during their afternoon prayers; after that, it was easier to understand why the Moroccans keep that French law. Only Muslims are permitted to enter the great mosque at Makkah.

Personal purity is required in order to perform many rituals, and is also acquired through performing certain rituals—purity of body, mind, and actions. Bathing, for Hindus, is preparation for performing most rituals, and is an important ritual act when performed in the Ganges, or at Cape Comorin, or Hardwar, or at Allahabad at the Great Mela, or at any convenient river, lake, or ocean on certain holy days. An Indian woman who had become a Christian leader in India once told me that on certain holidays when millions of Hindus are bathing in the waters of India, she joins them because the communal bathing binds all Indians together, quite apart from its religious significance. Hindu Sadhus who have renounced the world may establish their purity by bathing, or by covering their body with ashes, or by matting their hair with cowdung as a symbol of purification. Muslims are required to wash before saying their prayers and, when no water is available, may wash symbolically with sand or soil. The ritual of water purification is expected of everyone who enters a Shinto shrine. Physical purification as preparation for ritual worship includes removing shoes before entering mosques or most of the Asian temples.

In addition to bathing, the body must be purified for ritual worship by proper diet, by avoiding consumption of impurities that would make the performance of the ritual ineffective. For Hindus, eating beef makes a person impure; for Muslims, pork or shellfish are forbidden. Many Hindus and Buddhists and Jains are strict vegetarians.

Practice of purity in mind and action, that is, moral conduct, is both preparation for and the result of effective worship. Swamis often explained to me their belief that all religious ways agree on the basic moral practices needed in order to understand and follow a religious path: a person must be honest, kindly, considerate of others, generous, patient, diligent, sympathetic, and the like. Without commitment to making those characteristics habitual, efforts to live in awareness of truth, goodness, and beauty are unlikely to succeed. That is why Hindus have traditionally held that a young person should live with a guru until such moral conduct becomes habitual, before attempting education in religion, philosophy, or the arts. The Buddhists in Thailand, similarly, have required that those who are appointed to government positions must have lived for at least three months in a Buddhist monastery under the guidance of the Bhikkhus. The Islamic code of laws establishes the rules of conduct for all those who have submitted to Allah, conduct which makes it possible to understand and obey the divine commands revealed through Muhammad. The Jains have taught for many centuries that a precondition for worship is compassion, which includes avoidance of killing any creature; some Jains use masks to filter the air they breath lest they inadvertantly kill insects, so their every act might be compassionately considerate of all living things.

Charitable service to others may also be a ritual, and a preparation for other rituals. Hindus should support the temple and the priests and the Swamis and sadhus, and they should each day feed an animal and give something to a beggar—these are actions good in themselves, and also necessary clarifying preconditions for worship, for approaching the God, or Gods. Islamic law requires that the devout give a fixed percentage of their income to the mosque, and to the needy; the amount expected varies in different Islamic countries, but the obligation is on all Muslims. The ritual giving in Theravada Buddhist countries includes providing the food for Bhikkhus when they beg from door to door as their vows require; it also includes the support of temples and monasteries and of the needy. Throughout Asia the traditional religious rituals have encouraged members of the group to give to the support of their religious leaders and institutions, and to show compassion to the needy in their community.

Religious rituals play a significant role in shaping community life, and the life of each individual born into it. They have been created to remind followers of a religious path of their religious traditions and of the ways they are expected to act in order to win increased awareness of the world and increased ability to act in it for the good. Religious insights are maintained when they bring new insights and a sense of awe in fresh awareness of the realities in human experience, and when they reveal the possibility of living in greater harmony with others who are trying to help possible good to become actual.

Participation in rituals from an early age is a powerful influence in setting the path to be followed through a lifetime. For some, participation in rituals may be simply a yielding to social pressures, or even a means of manipulating the givens of one's surroundings for personal advantage. But religious ritual may also serve as a channel of communication with Sacred Reality, as a way of opening humans to religious insights and good choices, as a source of strength in time of distress, and as an expression of joy and gratitude for the given wonders of the world.

From earliest times, the communal celebration of cherished religious insights has inspired creativity in all the different arts: in architecture and gardens, the graphic arts and sculpture, in music, dance, imaginative literature and drama. Religious speculations concerning what humans hold to be true and good are expressed with reverent wonder through theology and philosophy and the natural and social sciences—and through all the arts by those followers of religious paths whose talents make such imaginative creativity possible. The exploration of religious paths other than one's own leads to intriguing discoveries of the myriad ways humans have expressed their wonder at what they find to be true and good and beautiful, and of the different ways communities of religious followers have accepted those expressions of religious insights.

Truly religious arts evoke a sense of wonder to which we react with a mixture of emotion, curiosity, and evaluation—a reaction skillfully shaped by the artist's insights into how things happen and ought to happen in the world. Some arts create objects that do not change—like an image, or painting, or building that can be apprehended in a moment. Other arts unfold in a passing stream of time: drama, dance, music, a narrative, a garden. These arts embody and illuminate religious insights perceived in the realities of human experience by followers of quite different religious paths. And the religious insights expressed in words, harmonious sounds, colors, textures, and shapes are perceived differently by different persons and by the same person at different times.

Religious art is created by devout followers of a religious path whose curiosity reaches beyond what *is* to what might be better, and whose unusual talents let them dare to express, within the limits of the materials available, the beauty, the possible harmony they have discovered. Religious art moves the observer toward the tranquillity and the self-forgetting sought as a condition for worship and insight. It illuminates ways to greater alertness to other persons, and to clearer understanding of the world outside the self. It helps us to see ourselves in perspective, to see how we might be in more harmonious relations with our surroundings. It stimulates a search for the true and the good by recalling or uncovering aspects of the sacred. Religious arts encourage a sense of wonder, awe, joy, gratitude, devotion, and hope in the face of disappointment and suffering.

Works of art that have played a role in ceremonies and ritual have a special sanctity from their part in shaping the lives of the community. Some art forms have been scorned by some religious communities, some simply ignored, some cherished for special occasions, some for private devotions. As symbols and as myths, religious arts have played significant roles in preserving and teaching religious traditions.

Drama, dance, and music all unfold over time, revealing their content and structure progressively. We appreciate the import of these performances as we experience the shifting relationships between the chosen significant elements—perhaps dramatic characters or dancers or instruments, perhaps themes or moods or rhythms. Our experience of performances, then, effectively parallels our experience of the real world of continuous change. But the creators of drama, dance, and music, be they innovators or strict traditionalists, present us with experiences framed and shaped so as to direct and focus our understanding (or, at least, our curiosity). Thus, these arts can play a powerful role in the adaptation of each individual to the outlook that is itself unfolding in the culture at any given time.

Dramatic religious presentations at a temple or mosque are not frequent today, but many staged dramas deal with religious issues. On one memorable occasion I spent an evening in Indonesia watching a community enactment of the pranks and loyalty of Hanuman, the Monkey God companion of the God Rama, performed by Muslims for an enthusiastic Muslim audience—such is the hold of a drama cherished by their Hindu forefathers some centuries ago.

Rather than as staged dramas for the artistically minded, much of the religious drama in Asia takes the form of religious rituals and ceremonies. Often, ordinary citizens "take roles" or enact the drama themselves. The daily prayers in a mosque, combining actions and spoken prayers, provide drama. The ceremonies of recognizing maturity, marriage, and death are drama—high drama in the funeral ceremonies for important people in Thailand. In Hindu temples, the consecrated image through which the God is worshiped often participates in an ongoing drama as the priests and worshipers, in the role of servants to a ruler, take the image daily through such events as waking, meals, and bathing; often great street festivals are an extension of this drama, wherein the God annually makes a procession among the homes of his people. Drama in all these forms stimulates new curiosity, insight and commitment, new joy and gratitude.

Without words, but often using music and costume as background, religious dance relies on the rhythmic blending of posture, gesture, and movement of the human body to express religious insights and devotion. Dance is often presented in Asia in carefully choreographed and costumed religious rituals.

In India, religious dance has been popular for centuries, with several major schools flourishing in different regions of the country. It begins with ritual preparation and is accompanied by religious music; its movements represent familiar religious images and paintings, dramatize stories from well-known religious writings. So the dance becomes a complex and moving presentation of the religious insights and devotion of the choreographer and dancer. Familiarity with the meanings of the mudras (hand gestures), the postures, and the stories being enacted, aids understanding. But it is a common experience that religious dance of India transcends language and tradition and can speak directly to followers of other religious traditions just as it has to Hindus for centuries. The influence of Indian dance is evident in Thailand, and in Indonesia, having persisted through many religious changes.

Many years ago when I was trying to understand the role of dance in Hindu religious practices, friends in Madras urged me to spend a morning at a dancing recital given by young girls who had been studying under a highly respected teacher. They explained that only recently had the Brahman community allowed their daughters to participate in a religious dance in public—it had usually been presented by devadasis at the temple. The girls performed their routines well, to the applause of their families, and then formed a half-circle for the teacher to come out. She was middle-aged, wearing an ordinary sari, and simply walked to the middle of the stage, stood there a moment, then made only a slight move and began to dance—it was an electric, dramatic, unexpected glimpse of the sacred! The teacher was Balasaraswati, one of the greatest dancers of this century.

Later, she told me that when she dances she can suggest the presence of a God, of Krishna for instance, by assuming part of the Krishna posture known from the familiar images—but never the complete imitation of the God lest she be stricken for arrogance. Religious dance is an art with remarkable power to create an awareness of sacred reality.

For some Muslims, the question as to whether or not dancing is permitted was determined by an event recorded in the Hadith: once, when the Prophet praised a follower, the man danced for joy—and since the Prophet did not rebuke him, it is agreed that a Muslim may dance. In Islam, dance has often been associated with Sufi orders, such as the ritual dance of the whirling dervishes which has been performed by the Mevlevis since the thirteenth century. It was forbidden under the secular reforms of Ataturk but when after a quarter of a century the prohibition was lifted, they discovered that the dance had been preserved secretly and passed on to the next generation as a cherished means of communication with Allah.

If rhythmic movements of hands and body to communicate meaning and emotions is dancing, then dance is a significant part of many rituals. In Islam, for instance, the daily prayers involve the ritual dance of standing, bowing, kneeling, and rising, repeated a fixed number of times—and to do that in harmony with dozens, or hundreds, or thousands of others, all facing toward Makkah, is a powerful unifying dance. In Hinduism, many of the acts of devotion require accompanying movements, such as circumambulation of the temple or image, bowing, making offerings, bathing the image. In Tibet the circumambulation might be made by repeated prostrations, moving one body-length at a time, sometimes for considerable distances; there are processions, bowings, offerings, all to be performed in prescribed ways. In Theravada Buddhism the Bhikkhus are taught to walk in a distinctive way as if it were a dance step, while wearing a distinctive robe. In Japan, the celebration of the birthday of the founder of a Buddhist temple may involve several hours of ceremonies including walking in procession, kneeling, bowing, making offerings, all while dressed in special robes for the occasion. At Shinto shrines, sometimes the dance is a breath-takingly beautiful expression of religious devotion.

Music, for many people, conveys awareness of the sacred and expresses wonder and gratitude that have only been hinted at in words. At Chidambaram (where some Hindus believe Natarajan first danced in joyful creation of the world) I once spent a couple of days in a pilgrim hostel as guest of a Brahman friend who had persuaded them to overlook my non-caste status. There I met a prosperous Indian lawyer who had come a considerable distance for his annual holiday at the temple to join with half a dozen friends for several days of singing together. As I sat by the doorway of a small temple, the only listener, and saw the devotion with which they sang, I realized that I was privileged to observe how music can express sincere religious insights and devotion. I have found similar awareness and reverence when Tibetan monks chant to the accompaniment of their drums and horns; and when, in Japan, I sat at the back of the room during ceremonies in Soto Zen, Rinzai Zen, and Nichiren temples, and at Shinto shrines; and when, in a mosque in Istanbul, I heard a Mullah chanting a passage from the *Qur'an* at Friday prayers.

Again and again as I listened to music sung, or chanted, or created by talented musicians on the vina, the sitar, the koto, the drums, the gongs, I heard religious music expressing sensitive understanding of human sufferings and joys, tenderness and compassion, yearning and gratitude. Sometimes music offers consolation, or encouragement, or inspiration, or new insights. Music as a means of worship expresses the relationship perceived between mankind and the holy—it may be prayer, or reaching out for greater awareness and ability to increase harmony in the world, or a spontaneous expression of joy and wonder. The recognition of the religious quality in music is most likely to come to those persons who have also been searching for it in visual arts, human actions, and writings.

All of the arts, of course, can have qualities other than those recognized here as religious. Music can be simply a device for releasing emotional tensions—refreshing, amusing, decorative, playful; it can be vulgar. It may be used to manipulate people by inducing conformity in crowds, or by creating emotions that lead to self-centeredness, to violence, to war. That the meanings expressed in music can have social significance has been shown in this generation by the efforts of dictatorial governments in Asia to control the music that could be heard in China, Japan, the Soviet Union, and Turkey in times of war and revolution. When music is used as a means of manipulation, used to create moods of conformity to patterns of conduct set by a religious organization or a guru, it loses its religious quality and becomes only sounds designed to keep people in step. Quite apart from the possibility that music, like the other arts, can be and often is misused, it is enough to point out that religious music can be an effective technique for becoming aware of sacred realities and for expressing religious insights.

Similarly, in the literary arts of poetry and stories, words are used in ways that express more than their literal content. In poetry, for example, words are pre-structured in formal patterns, such as in lines with unvarying formal characteristics. Such formal patterns permit meaningful relationships to be brought out by such devices as juxtaposition of paired line-endings or sound-echoes like rhyme. Figurative language also is a common poetic and narrative device; the audience is drawn into involvement, having actively to provide, under direction, a portion of the meaning that has been indicated but not stated. The imaginative and creative use of words expresses religious insights that may be perceived with sensitive awareness (as do the other arts that communicate through sounds, colors, shapes, and movement).

Jalaluddin Rumi, the great master of Islamic mystical poetry, uses verbal images and symbols taken from human experience to tell in poetry, stories, and parables of the path of longing and love that leads to God. Since the thirteenth century his writings have been influential in the Persian-speaking world, and in translation in Turkey, Pakistan, India, and in more recent times in Europe and America. Among Muslims, particularly those who are skillful in Arabic and Persian, poetry has often been the art form chosen for expressing religious aspiration, wonder, gratitude, and devotion to Allah, and His Prophets. Often these poets have bemoaned their inability, even using every device available, to express in words the marvels of the sacred. In popular devotional Hinduism, the reciting and singing of poetry is as common as traditional ritual acts involving sacred places or objects. Friends in southern India often pointed out to me their belief that the Buddhists of their part of India returned from their heretical ways to Hinduism when they were charmed by hearing the Alvars recite and sing their ecstatic poetry in praise of God.

Narrative literature also has its distinctive and imaginative ways of reaching and affecting the audience, of saying what is real, good, sacred. For example, in Hinduism some parts of the *Mahabharata* and *Ramayana* have the status of sacred writings about the heavens, the Gods, the cycles of earthly existence, and other parts are cherished as poetry and stories that have shaped the religious life of the community. Personification is powerful in the epic narratives, as Vishnu appears in person, and leading characters embody particular virtues like loyalty. The *Jataka Tales* of the previous existences of the Buddha have influenced Buddhist thought and practice for centuries. Allegory also often plays a role in religious narrative, as when the sighing of the gopis after the beautiful prince Krishna is understood to show the longing of the soul for union with God. All religious groups in Asia treasure narratives about remarkable persons in their traditions and about supernatural beings and events that have captured the imaginations and motivated the followers of their religious path.

The great Hindu epics, for instance, have been well-known throughout Asia for centuries, often in local versions, providing a vast cultural common ground that extends even across religious boundaries. The stories about the divine monkey have delighted many generations of people who have grown up hearing about Hanuman, the embodiment of loyalty and courageous faithfulness to the God Rama, and about Wu-k'ung the miraculous monkey companion and protector of Hsuan-tsang on his pilgrimage from China to India to procure Buddhist Sutras. The stories about Hanuman and Wu-k'ung are known today in paintings, books, comic books, films, and plays, entertaining young and old. For some, the stories are only amusing accounts of the actions of delightful superhuman beings; for others, they are reminders that Hanuman and Wu-k'ung are resourceful divine pranksters who show us that joy, playfulness and fun are part of the experience of the holy, that—in spite of faults and failures—loyalty and courage in the service of a good cause can ultimately bring about good results.

The stories about Hanuman in the *Ramayana* have been treasured for many centuries as a classic Hindu epic, even as a scripture. The image of Hanuman is the representation of a Hindu God who is the embodiment of loyalty and devotion to Rama, as is evident when an observer at a Hindu temple or home sees the sincere expressions of devotion at a shrine where Hanuman is worshiped. In China, *The Journey to the West* (four volumes in the English translation of the book written in the sixteenth century C.E.) records the antics of the monkey Wu-k'ung in poetry and prose that includes many subtle critical comments on sectarian differences of Buddhism, Taoism, and Confucianism in China—comments often missed by contemporary readers.

Numerous examples are available to show how poetry and imaginative narrative writings have shaped Asian religious ideas about the real and the sacred, and have inspired ritual and communal religious life in Asia.

In religious arts, calligraphy is the link between literature and painting, sculpture, and architecture, enhancing the communicative power of words by reinforcing their inherent meanings with significant visual form. The art of calligraphy has been raised to exquisite expressive heights in the preparation with loving care of holy texts, and in the adornment of homes, mosques, shrines, and temples. The calligraphy may be a word of admonition or inspiration, or a quotation from a revered teacher or from a sacred writing. It may serve as a starting point for worship or for religious meditation, for instance: "OM" in Hinduism, "Om Mani Padme Hum" in Tibetan Buddhism, "Namu Amida Butsu" or "Namu Myoho-renge-kyo" in Japanese Buddhism. Or, it may be a reminder of the way a follower of a religious path aspires to act. A Muslim scholar in Cairo had on the wall of his study the word "Patience," because, he said, it is the first requirement for following the Straight Path of Islam. A Zen Roshi, famous in Japan for his calligraphy, when asked for a work of calligraphic art that would be a guide to the way of Zen, inscribed "Unattached Like a Cloud."

In classical Sanskrit, Chinese, Japanese, and Arabic, religious calligraphy is an important form of religious art expressing insight and devotion. In all languages and scripts, calligraphy that presents religious insights as works of art is cherished for the instruction and inspiration it brings to meditation and worship.

Paintings have been forbidden in some traditions and cherished in others as reminders of religious teachings, as a means of communicating religious insights for which words are inadequate, as a stimulus for religious meditation, and as objects of devotion and inspiration.

Devout followers of Islam have usually looked with disfavor on any representations of human or animal figures that might become objects of devotion. Although their religious arts are limited to geometric forms, the natural world, plants, and sometimes stylized animals, the proportions of their designs in the graphic arts often express an awareness of the order, complexity, and beautiful harmony of reality seen as created by Allah, and therefore sacred. In the other traditions, creative imagination is as free in creating religious paintings as in all the other arts—influenced, but not necessarily restricted by the culture of the artists.

Pictures of founders or favorite teachers, either as portraits or when performing some memorable act, are cherished reminders in many religious communities. Once, when I asked the Chinese headmaster of a Confucian school what he recommends as a reminder for students, expecting him to suggest a favorite calligraphic word or quotation, he showed me a picture of Confucius such as he wants each of his students to have. The drawing of Bodhidharma standing so light in the world that he can cross the river on a straw, or the ten oxherding pictures showing how the passions can be tamed, are examples of Zen pictures designed for instruction in the aims of the religious community. The symbols used to express religious insights, such as the lotus, the trident, the Zen circle, crescent, the lion, the crane, serve as reminders and stimulus for meditation, and as objects of devotion.

Tibetan thangkhas are examples of paintings that are sacred because they are used as objects of devotion, as reminders of religious traditions, and as inspiration for actions that are harmonious with what has been discovered to be true and good. Thangkhas, painted on cloth in bright colors, combine pictures of Buddhas, or Bodhisattvas, or celestial beings, or revered teachers, with familiar symbols, all in traditional formal patterns. Often they have an attached cover-cloth which is raised when the thangkha is an object of meditation or worship and then is reverently dropped.

Once, in Kalimpong, a Tibetan artist who had recently come from Lhasa was commissioned by a Tibetan friend to create a thangkha for me. After a long discussion about what it should include, they decided the central figure should be the Buddha in the posture of giving instruction, with celestial beings in the four corners (chosen as appopriate guardians and guides for me), and completed with such symbols and traditional designs as the artist found fitting. My Tibetan friends explained that there are eight auspicious symbols commonly used in Tibetan paintings: the umbrella represents protection from hindrances and suffering; two golden fish symbolize freedom from restraints; a vase is a container of treasures fulfilling highest aspirations; the lotus symbolizes purity of body, speech, and mind; a conch shell symbolizes the sounding of the Dharma which awakens all beings from the sleep of ignorance and calls them to actions benefiting all beings; the endless knot symbolizes the interdependence of all things and the interaction between wisdom and compassion; the victory banner symbolizes the overcoming of all obstacles to enlightenment, and the victory of the Buddha Dharma; the wheel symbolizes the continuing turning throughout the universe of the wheel of the teachings and insights of the Buddha.

The use of three dimensional images to represent deities or persons as objects of devotion is forbidden in Islam, and is controversial among many of the followers of other Asian paths. Some of them disapprove because it seems to them that a material object has been deified; or because the myths or symbols represented are unknown or misunderstood or rejected; or simply because they think images distract from or impede religious insight. Those who use images in their religious devotions, on the other hand, do so because they find that images, as is the case with other religious arts, are for some people a most effective way to express, or discover, religious insights.

When I was living in Hindu ashrams many years ago, the Swamis took great pains to explain to me that worship before an image must begin with prayers inviting the God to come again into the consecrated image while the devotee worships, and that afterwards the God is dismissed. The image is temporarily a material representation toward which worship may be directed. Because the image has served as a symbol in worship, it is respected, sacred—just as any place where humans have worshiped is treated with affectionate respect and reverence. One of the Swamis, to make that point, told of his recent experience when he and another Swami were walking on a pilgrimage to Allahabad at the time of the mela, the gathering of hundreds of thousands of devout Hindus at the sacred place where the Jumna and Ganges rivers come together. As they approached the city they saw an old woman bowing before the three mile marker, offering flowers and Ganges water. The Swami spoke to her, "Mother, that is not a Shiva lingam, that is only a stone marker put there by the British raj to show that it is three miles to the city. That symbol on the stone is not OM, but the way the British write the number three." She replied, "To you, it may be a British mile post, to me it is Shiva, it is OM." The Swami said he went on his way, shamed.

Some of the Swamis explained their embarrassment at what they considered the prudery of outsiders who misinterpret the Shiva lingam as a representation of the penis, and therefore consider the Swamis tasteless and vulgar idolators (as the Swamis would themselves consider anyone who worshiped a phallic symbol). They said it is likely that in ancient times there were some people who saw the Shiva lingam as a phallic symbol, but for centuries true devotees have revered the lingam as the ideal abstract, impersonal symbol of Shiva, the Creative Power back of all that exists, a Power that cannot be limited to a personal form. It is for Shiva's devotees the pure, abstract symbol for God, just as the salagrama (a small, black river-rounded stone from a sacred river) symbolizes the living presence of Vishnu. The Swamis said that only those persons who have been so dominated by their sexual fantasies that they see most symbols as having sexual significance could have misunderstood the Shiva lingam.

The Swamis were also enthusiastic about certain other representations of Shiva in a personal form, images that managed to convey some if not all of the God's remarkable qualities. The Shiva Natarajan, the Dancing Shiva, one of the most beautiful of the Hindu images, is a personification of the same God represented by the lingam, an image specially emphasizing several of God's powers. Devout Swamis enjoyed explaining to me that the Dancing Natarajan is God dancing in the sheer joy of creation: all other explanations of how and why the world was created can be dismissed as speculation, but that the act of creation was a joyful divine dance is shown by the overwhelming diversity and complexity and beauty of the heavens, the earth and growing things, including humans who love and laugh and cry and also, on occasion, sing and dance for joy. In another image, the androgynous Shiva represents God as one-half male and one-half female, going beyond the limitation of imagining God as either He or She.

During the early centuries of their tradition, the Buddhists as a reforming, heretical group breaking away from Hinduism judged it improper to make images of the Buddha, referring to the Buddha visually only through conventional symbols like the deer or the wheel of the law. But after a few centuries they began creating beautiful images representing the Buddha, the Buddhas, the Bodhisattvas, and outstanding Buddhist teachers as personifications of Buddhist teachings about reality and the Path to be followed by all humans. Some Buddhists hear with horror, and some with amusement, the story of the Chinese Ch'an monk who, on a cold morning when there was no fuel for a fire, broke up and burned a wooden image of the Buddha, making his point that it was only a piece of wood. Images of the walking Buddha celebrate the beauty of the human figure, while seated images of the laughing and plump Bodhisattva are reminders of blessings and the joy of living. At Angkor and at many other shrines, the Bodhisattva Avalokitesvara looks out in all directions in compassion. At many

Buddhist shrines (particularly in Cambodia and at Borobudur and Nara and Kyoto) the images show the calm, the
tranquillity, that is sought as preparation for meditation and
worship. In other images, the number of arms—even suggesting a thousand-armed figure—are accepted as symbols
for the many powers attributed to the Bodhisattva. The
gestures of the images are effective reminders of Buddhist
teachings: hand up with palm outward, have no fear; fingers touching the earth, our strength comes from the earth;
palm up in the gesture of giving, a reminder of how much
has been given to us; hands together in the lap, meditation
which is the way to enlightenment.

Images (and calligraphy and paintings) have the advantage that they can be large or small, can be moved from
place to place, can be in a cell or a home, in a park or along
a highway, may adorn a public building, may be the central
object in a shrine. In the communities where religious images are treasured, they are a constant reminder of the religious paths to which some members of the community are
committed.

Most communities throughout the world have a building, or buildings, set aside for religious purposes. Thus, a
sacred place, a place for devotion provided by members of
the community, is one of the givens of human experience. A
building is a work of religious art when it has been created to
be a beautiful place for worship, and becomes sacred when
worship has been performed there repeatedly. The place may
have been chosen because an event of religious importance
happened there, or because of its association with a revered
person, or because of its natural beauty, or simply for convenience. In most Asian traditions the buildings provide a
setting for group worship, for instruction, for housing persons who devote full time to religious activities, and for
presenting to the public the religious arts approved by the
persons responsible for the rituals performed there.

As with the other arts, exploring the religious architecture created by followers of the religious paths of Asia

increases awareness of the variety, the creative originality, the devotion, the sense of the nearness of the sacred that is found again and again in the religious communities of Asia.

There is an overwhelming variety in the mosques from Morocco on the Atlantic, through Kairouan in Tunisia, Cairo, Saudi Arabia, Damascus, Istanbul, Baghdad, Karbala, Najaf, Tehran, Isfahan, Lahore, Delhi, Kuala Lumpur, to Indonesia on the Pacific. I knew I would not be welcomed in Makkah, but was surprised not to be allowed to enter mosques in Morocco, or at Kairouan, or in some mosques in Iraq and Iran. Otherwise I was free to visit the mosques at will, to observe services of worship, and to marvel at the beauty of the design and adornment that had been created with loving care and originality, with devoted spontaneity within strict limits.

I once visited Santa Sophia in Istanbul with a Muslim friend who as a boy had been brought there many times by his father for daily prayers when it was a mosque. Now we were visiting a museum where tourists paid admission and moved noisily about, and it was forbidden to have any religious service in the building. Some of the Islamic calligraphy remained, some of the Christian mosaics were recently restored while others were still under reconstruction. Both of us were moved by the wonder of the building and the art— the awesome upthrust and encompassing space of the immense dome, and the beauty of the graphic adornments from the two related but so different traditions. Both of us wished that it could still be a place of worship, even if only in one little side chapel as a mosque and another as a church. For both of us, the wonders of the building transcended the barriers of our society.

The varied artistry of Hindu temples, shrines, and monasteries has been developing for thousands of years, revered by myriad generations of devout Hindus. Characteristically, the central shrine of a place of worship is a small area in the center of the structure, a sacred spot with room for only a few people to worship at a time, as at Chidambaram where the Dancing Natarajan image is enshrined. The rest of the structure, which may include an extensive complex of passageways and courtyards, will be adorned with many images, with bas reliefs, with decorative symbols and designs. A small temple such as Halebid, in southern India, sits on a massive stone base, rising above it barely enough to permit entry standing erect—the roof outside, and the ceiling inside, are essentially flat. The interior is dark and broken into rooms and alcoves, in which the powerful images appear to be confined away from the outside world. The building is covered with images inside and out.

Hindu devotion is expressed through circumambulating and walking through a temple, by offering prayers and gifts before the central shrine and before the other images in the temple compound. When a large crowd assembles, the people gather in the courtyard, or a nearby open area. Over the centuries, the beautiful temples of India have been built by devout Hindus who chose to express their religious insights through architecture adorned with fitting images—temples which have endured for as long as there have been people who shared those insights, who chose to worship there. Sometimes, when the insights are no longer shared, the buildings or the images are preserved simply because they are beautiful, or because they were once seen as sacred.

Buddhist architecture began with the stupa, a burial mound containing a relic of the Buddha. Sanchi, in India, is an early example, now prized as a work of art. Stupas have been built as places of devotion in many Buddhist communities; perhaps the most elaborate is the one at Borobudur in Indonesia, now a Buddhist monument in an Islamic country. The stupa, over centuries, became in some countries a pagoda. A Burmese Bhikkhu once explained to me that the Shwedagon Pagoda in Rangoon has the best vibrations for meditation and worship of any place in the world. The pagodas in Nepal, China, and Japan became a devoutly elaborated architectural design rising several tiers, sometimes having a room with an image, with other buildings for community gatherings nearby. In addition to the stupa, caves have been sacred structures in Buddhism, notably at Ajanta in India, Bamiyan in Afghanistan and Dunhuang in China. They were adorned with paintings, bas reliefs, and images of remarkable artistic and inspiring quality. Buddhist temples are often the most beautiful buildings in the community, whether they be the gorgeously decorated temples of Thailand, the awe-inspiring architecture of Angkor Wat in Cambodia, the massive Potala in Lhasa, or the beautiful temples and monasteries of China and Japan.

In all but the most isolated communities, from the Mediterranean to the Pacific, all people in the community are exposed to architecture created as an expression of religious devotion to provide a place where what is seen as sacred can be worshiped. When we think of how little we know about all the different mosques, temples, pagodas, shrines, ashrams, monasteries, churches, and synagogues there are in our human commmunities, and of how little we know about the different religious insights expressed through those buildings, and about the ways they have been used, we realize that all of us need to be exploring religious ways other than our own in order that we can learn from each other and live more harmoniously together.

There is one more art to be considered as a given of community living that has religious significance: gardening. Some would say that a garden is a branch of architecture, or should be. Certainly it is sometimes an integral part of a religious architectural plan, as in a Zen temple or a Shinto shrine, but it may stand alone as an independent work of religious art. At the temple gardens in Kyoto I found that (as with religious art or music) it took many visits before I began to grasp what the artist was telling me. After a while, I found it interesting to observe the people who visited the gardens: for some of them it seemed to be only a time of rest, or of curiosity, or of aesthetic appreciation, but for others it was a time of devotion with the same rapt attention I had observed in temple services and in mosques.

A garden may be an expression of religious insight into the wonder and beauty of growing plants, and an exploration of the possibilities for natural beauty that can be realized through human efforts to create harmonious patterns from living things as they grow and unfold through time. Part of the wonder of the garden comes from the realization that humans can make many changes in the kinds of plants that grow together, and in the places where they grow, but it is always within the given limits of the place, the soil, the sunshine and water available, the seasonal changes, the timing. A garden challenges us with the mystery of the perils, frustrations, and joys of the brief cycles of birth, growth, aging, and death. A garden reminds us that all animals depend on plants for their existence, that when we select and plant and cultivate and watch we are altering and watching processes that are basic to all life. And when what grows is beautiful we realize that we did not create it, we just helped to make it possible within the given limits we did not set.

Five

Some Asian Ways of Following a Religious Path

Once in Cairo, when I was discussing the Day of Judgment with a professor who was widely respected as a rightly-guided Shaikh, he was surprised by my questions and exclaimed, "Why, if there were no Day of Judgment there would be no religion!" For him, the Day of Judgment is one of many given realities to be faced by every human who lives for a time on this planet. Just as death is inevitable for everyone, he said, it is inevitable that after death each person will be judged and punished for evil acts and rewarded for good acts. He went on to explain that Allah is just and therefore has revealed all that humans need to know in order to conform to the given realities, to the true, the good, and the Sacred in the world. To follow the Straight Path of Islam, according to the Shaikh, is to react to whatever happens in daily life in ways that will be approved by divine justice.

Thus far, what has been written here has dealt with what different Asian religious teachers say are the realities all humans face. They tell us that the given realities setting the limits for human choices are the realities of the natural processes of our planet, the realities seen as Sacred, and the realities of social pressures and guidance in the communities where people live.

Teachers in various religious groups in Asia tell us that back of all that exists is the reality that shapes our lives: a supreme God, or many Gods, or no deities; or there is a Sacred Mystery, a Divine Order, or a process that makes the good possible. Some religious leaders tell us there are many superhuman beings who are capable of altering the realities that limit human choices. Others say that what humans desire, and what they accomplish, is controlled by karma, or wu-wei, or ahimsa. They also tell us that there is a heaven and a hell, or many heavens and hells; that each human has a soul, or does not have a soul, and after death there is transmigration, or rebirth, or divine judgment determining eternal existence.

In Asia in our time, we are told that truths about those given realities, and about how humans should react to them, are discovered through experience guided by revelations from a divine source, or guided by insights of superior persons. Those truths are transmitted in writings or orally, in rituals, and through the arts.

The pilgrim who chooses to follow a religious path day after day through the complex and demanding given realities of life tries to follow that path as wisely, harmoniously, and compassionately as possible. Wisely: distinguishing between illusion and reality and discovering which given realities can be modified by human efforts. Harmoniously: finding mutually beneficial ways to bring the good into reality. Compassionately: helping the good that is possible in the circumstances to become actual.

When I asked my Asian aquaintances how to follow a religious path, I found general agreement (with many variations in emphasis and content) on the need to participate regularly in the rituals of group devotion and at the same time to experiment with other more individually oriented ways to improve one's own understanding and behavior.

Many Asians, in fact, emphasized the personal disciplines, assuming that the necessity for joining in worship with others would be obvious. Personal experiments in meditation and worship and good actions are necessary, they said, for anyone who is following traditional religious ways.

When I was studying Asian religious ways, I was drawn to people who were trying to comprehend more clearly the given realities of human existence. I looked for people whose concerns were centered outside themselves, for people who, like the Jains, sought to attain some measure of "freedom from disgust," people who were curious, sensitively aware, open and good-natured, and who pushed their search beyond the current cultural forms of their times, toward the edges of possible human outreach. As I look back, I confess to a lack of interest in the views of those persons who apparently followed a religious path only because it was customary, or pleasant, or expedient within the cultural pattern they preferred, or would provide rewards here or hereafter.

In Asia I asked many religious leaders what instructions should be given to a person who asks how to follow a religious path. The following selections from the answers given by devout seekers who are admired within their own cultures (and by me) show something of the similarities and incompatibilities, the multiplicity and diversity of the instructions they give with assurance.

I reported above in some detail what Gandhi said when I asked him how a student might go about trying to know whether there is a God. He said that the student would need to follow certain disciplines for several years. These include: control of the body; a limited vegetarian diet; extended periods of meditation while seated in the lotus posture and using mantras such as OM for insight and Ram (as the name of God) for devotion; acts of service to others, including some physical labor. He also recommended daily participation in group worship, using scriptures, singing, and prayers (often from Hindu, and Islamic, and Christian traditions).

Some thirty years after my talk with Gandhi, in Saigon during the Vietnamese-American war, I had an opportunity for an extended discussion with Thich Tri Quang, a leading Thien Buddhist monk, whose opposition to the war kept him in disfavor with both the Vietnamese and American officials. He received me at An Quang pagoda with chilly reserve, for he had become used to American efforts to manipulate him into supporting the war effort and was only seeing me because a mutual friend had asked him to. But when he found that the questions were about Buddhism, rather than politics, he became warmly friendly and answered without hesitation. He went out of his way to make it clear that the Thien Buddhism of Vietnam, even though it is in the Ch'an tradition from China, must not be confused with Ch'an or Zen—it is Thien, and Vietnamese. I asked Tri Quang what answer should be given to a student from the Buddhist University who had long ago given up all interest in Buddhism, but who recently has come to admire a friend who says that the kind of person the student admires has taken refuge in the Buddha. If a student were to ask him how to discover and understand the Buddha Dharma, how to follow the Path of the Buddha, what advice would Tri Quang give?

Tri Quang said that to follow the path of the Buddha three things are necessary: sincerity, a desire to be good, and a balance of body and mind. These three, in turn, make it possible to practice the meditation that leads to insight, the kind of insight that shapes the life of the person the student admires.

The first step, which requires sincerity, is taken by simply sitting quietly and recalling everything one did the day before. Everyone who does that will always recall some thoughts and actions with shame, and shame makes us want to do better, to be good. The desire to be good is our true nature—but this is often obscured in daily routines. The sincere desire to do better today is reinforced by the daily practice of recalling what one thought and did yesterday. (It is a desire to be better than we were, not to be better than someone else.) And it becomes clear that when our actions have expressed compassion there is no shame, that beauty in things or in actions is simply an expression of caring, of compassion.

At this stage of wanting to be good, some progress can be made if the seeker relies only on books and critical observations for guidance, but that is possible only for a very special person—for most people a teacher is needed, the instruction needs to be person to person. Once there is a sincere desire for good thoughts and actions, the third step must be taken: the development of balanced control of body and mind. This is necessary in order to stop flitting about and tiring the body and mind, to quiet both so the seeker becomes patient, self-controlled, and finally, tranquil. At this point a teacher is helpful because instruction is needed in the tested methods for controlling the puzzling interrelations of one's mind and body.

The first step in gaining a balance of body and mind, Tri Quang said, is proper breathing. At first, count the breath, one count for in and out, and do it ten times, and then ten times ten times; do this exercise three times a day at the same time each day. When the student has become more advanced, the breath is not counted because the rhythm has been established. When breathing out, imagine that all the wickedness of the self is being poured out, and when breathing in think of breath as purifying, cleansing. The second step in breathing is designed to calm the body by breathing as far down as possible—as if filling the whole body—sometimes through the mouth and sometimes through the nose, and always while facing east. (The reason for facing east was not explained, he said, but the Buddha taught that one should sleep on the right side with the head toward the east.) The third step in breathing is to take breaths as shallow as possible, a necessary condition for meditation. When a student is meditating, the teacher can tell by the

lightness of the breath whether or not the student is properly prepared for the meditation. The aim in controlling
the breath is to rid the body of diseases, to have a healthy,
calm body. It is strange, said Thich Tri Quang, but from
ancient times to now no one denies that proper breathing
gets rid of diseases—but to accomplish that we need a quiet
and serene life. Meditation is done without counting the
breath, but meditation is not possible without preliminary
breath control disciplines, he said.

Over the years, as I moved around in Asia, I asked the
same question, rephrasing it to fit the circumstances: when
someone asks you how to take initiative in following your
religious path, what do you suggest?

A Madrasi Brahman said you simply find a guru and
do what he commands. Several other Hindus found this
simple and direct answer sufficient and appropriate to the
question. Sri Krishna Menon, who at the time I saw him
was highly venerated in South India, said to find a guru
and submit to him (implying that he was the guru to whom
I should submit). Swami Ranganathananda said that the
religious search is for the appropriate guru to whom one
can submit with unswerving loyalty. Swami Hirananda
said that advice for following a religious path cannot be
given until a competent person has determined the spiritual level of the seeker; there is no one formula; everyone
must follow the counsel of an able guru who discerns the
disciplines that are fitting for that person at that time, just
as flowers grow if they are properly cultivated.

Hindus generally stressed this need for a wise personal
counselor; some went further, and mentioned the practices
that should be adopted under the direction of a competent
adviser. A teacher of yoga said that all we need to know has
been given us by Patanjali, that sincere seekers who learn
yoga from a guru who has mastered Patanjali's instructions
will then have the skills needed for controlling the body
and mind and directing all actions toward the true religious
goal. Sri Srinivasacharya, a devout retired business man

who had been a follower of Shankara's absolute monism and changed to Ramanuja's qualified monism after reading William James, said that the way to true insight is to practice yoga under the guidance of a competent teacher, and to follow the *Dharmashastras* as the laws guiding proper conduct. Dr. Raghavan said that when starting on the religious way the first step is to ask the help of a wise teacher; then sit still and think, working to clear one's mind. A dark room at midnight is a good place for such efforts because it is free from distractions. Religious meditation is helped by observing nature, by listening to music, and by recalling a verse or two of scripture as a measure to be used in examining oneself. Chanting the name of God and reciting approved mantras scours the mind. There should be an hour of altruistic work every day, such as in a hospital or with people in need, to free oneself from selfish ties.

In Islamic communities the answers indicated that guidance for conduct is to be sought from the consensus of religious leaders, rather than from an individual guru. Only in Tehran was the advice often given that a beginning student should submit to a personal teacher—in order to clean the dust from the mirror and catch the light that is seen through the commonly expected daily prayers and proper conduct. While the Hindus usually left most discretion to the guru, Muslims usually mentioned specific texts and rituals as guides.

In Turkey, I was told that followers of the Straight Path of Islam must obey the shari'a, the laws of conduct as interpreted by the Muslim leaders recognized in the community as rightly-guided. In Iran, the Shi'i authority for the laws of conduct is the *Qur'an*, as illuminated by the traditions of the Prophet, and as interpreted by the Imams and by those present-day leaders who have demonstrated outstanding piety, justice, and administrative ability. It is necessary to submit to such leaders as the guides given for these times. In Cairo at Al Azhar University, several of the Shaikhs spent some time making sure that I had heard their dependable exposition of the basic requirements for following the Straight Path of Islam. They said the first step is to seek the advice of the Ulama (the rightly-guided leaders, as they considered themselves to be) and under their guidance learn to obey Islamic law and customs, to study the sacred texts and perform the daily prayers.

Throughout the world of Islam, memorized passages from the *Qur'an* and the Hadith (the remembered words and actions of Muhammad) are frequently recited as a form of worship, like the daily prayers. Some of the Ulama and many Sufis also recommend that worship should include dhikr, that is, remembering God by ritualistic repetition of glorifying names and phrases. In Indonesia, a Shaikh whose large following revered him as a Sufi, told me that every day, in addition to the daily prayers and recitation of passages from the *Qur'an*, a Muslim should dhikr, which he described as kneeling as in the prayers with the back straight and repeating "Allah" over and over hundreds of times, pronouncing clearly with the breath going out on "ah."

When I asked what Islamic writings are recommended in addition to the *Qur'an* and the Hadith, sometimes I was looked upon with suspicion and sometimes I received enthusiastic recommendations. In Turkey, the writings of Rumi are widely known through public recitations on radio and in public gatherings, and commended to students of Islam. In Iran the writings of Ali and of several of the Imams are frequently offered as sources of inspiration and guidance. The Egyptian Shaikhs had fewer reservations about al-Ghazali as a supplement to their instructions than about any other Islamic writer.

Whatever the local customs may be, a follower of the Straight Path joins with all true Muslims in the daily prayers, without regard for such class or racial distinctions as may exist in the community. A social distinction widely observed at daily prayers in the mosque is that if women choose to join in the daily prayers, they are kept separate from the men.

The Buddhists of South Asia, like the Hindus, generally stressed the crucial importance of attaching oneself to a wise teacher. Other common emphases for the religious seeker are moral conduct and achieving tranquillity of mind—necessary preliminaries to meditation and insight. Bhikkhu Kashyap, for example, who moved from his Hindu background to become a leader of Theravada Buddhism in India, said that the first step for a Buddhist is to take the Five Precepts (I accept the precept not to kill, not to steal, not to commit any sexual misconduct, not to lie, and not to take any intoxicating liquor or drug), and then to seek tranquillity by learning to relax, to sit still, and to watch one's breath. After that, it becomes possible to move toward understanding and following the Buddhist path under a good teacher. The Vice-Chancellor of Vidyodaya University in Sri Lanka, some years ago, said that everyone must start by seeking out a good teacher, just as you would seek a good physician if ill, and that teacher will show how to meditate, which is the way to be a Buddhist. U Thittila, a distinguished Theravada teacher in Rangoon, said that following the path is possible for those who find a good teacher to guide their conduct and meditation. Bhikkhu Sasana Sobhana Maha Thera in Bangkok said, and other Bhikkhus there agreed with him, that the first step is to find a guru and to practice moral precepts under the guru's guidance—then it becomes possible to learn how to meditate, and to learn the Dhamma. Phra Dhammarama, who was a senior professor at the Buddhist University in what was then Cambodia, said that at the start it is necessary to go to the temple eight times a month for regular instructions, then to select a teacher and to learn how to meditate, beginning with the breathing exercises.

In Vietnam, Thich Thien Hoa said that the seeker must find a teacher in order to learn how to follow the Buddhist rules for conduct, must learn to pray in order to calm the mind, and then can turn to meditation under the guidance of the teacher. Another monk there stressed the need to calm the body, to be able to sit still, and for that it is important to control the diet by avoiding spices, meat, eggs, and milk: only then could instruction be given with some hope of success. A Buddhist layman in Vietnam agreed that control of the body is the first step, requiring a vegetarian diet, no alcohol or drugs. Then the seeker should use such disciplines for quieting the mind as counting beads, or fingers, or centering attention on a beautiful flower, or picture, or image. When you have learned to empty the mind of uncontrolled thoughts, then it is possible to meditate. Another Buddhist layman, who had helped create a modern temple and had participated in several international Buddhist gatherings, said that since there are many types of people, skillful Buddhist teachers adjust to their differences—some are by nature devotional, others active, or meditative, or mystical. Most of the followers of the Path of the Buddha need to have teachers who can give them appropriate instructions in how to meditate, how to breathe properly, and how to control their thoughts, examine their actions of the previous day and put into practice their inevitable resolves to do better today.

In Taiwan, a layman in the Ch'an tradition said that a competent Ch'an master will start instruction in how to follow the Path of the Buddha by rousing in the seeker a sense of wonder—wonder about time and transiency, about the complexities and order and beauty in the world around us. The problem is to find ways to awaken people to wonder and to help them develop the skills needed for exploring the wonders they discover.

In Japan, devout followers of Nichiren said that the true religious path is made clear in the *Lotus Sutra* and a devotee follows that path by honoring Nichiren's calligraphic representation of the title of the Sutra and by repeating with devotion "*Namu Myoho-renge-kyo*" (*I honor* [or trust, or take refuge in, or devote myself to] the *Sutra of the Lotus of the Wonderful Truth*). Other Japanese friends, followers of the Shinshu path, advised that we cannot follow a religious path in these times by our own efforts, that we must recognize human weakness and put complete trust in the Other-Power by repeating the Nembutsu: "Namu Amida Butsu." The sacred phrase does not translate successfully, but expresses complete trust in the Buddha and in the promise of enlightenment for those who have that trust. Devout repetition of the Nembutsu strengthens the trust in the Other-Power that will help the devotee to escape from the frustrations and disappointments of this present existence. The late Shibayama Roshi, a Rinzai Zen Master, said religious insight comes person-to-person so each seeker must have a master capable of giving instruction fitted to that person's needs, a master capable of examining the disciple's progress, of imposing appropriate disciplines of conduct, study, and meditation—and of recognizing when a pilgrim along the way of Zen has attained satori.

When I talked with followers of tantra, some of them expounded their belief that tantra is the highest form of religious practice, open to followers of any tradition who have risen to the elite heights that make it possible to follow their teachings. They found it would be impossible for me to understand tantra because I had not progressed far enough in religious insight to receive tantric instructions. That I had not progressed far enough must have been clear to them as they saw how my attention wandered when they talked about their esoteric accomplishments, about tantra as a short-cut to religious insight by means of difficult secret practices, or about the manipulation of material objects as a way to gain religious insight.

Sometimes Hindus would tell me that tantra is not part of the truly Vedic traditions, but a separate cult occasionally adopted by Hindus. One devout Hindu teacher, honored as a pandit in his community, warned that following tantra is like trying to walk barefoot on the edge of a sword, that the tantric efforts to demonstrate freedom from attachment to material pleasures were often self-destructive. Buddhists often said that tantra is not Buddhist but is a cult that might be found among some persons who follow Buddhist traditions. Tibetan Buddhist friends have patiently explained to me that tantra is religious insight transmitted through special symbols that can be understood only after years of disciplined preparation under the guidance of superior religious teachers. I have not had such disciplined training, nor sought it, but I have known and admired Tibetan Buddhists who have chosen to undergo tantric training.

Enough of examples of Asian answers to questions about how to follow a religious path. Running through the advice from religious leaders of many Asian traditions was the suggestion that seekers must take initiative in the difficult, life-long process of developing skills needed in order to follow a religious path. Those skills include techniques of preparation that "clean the dust from the mirror," that develop tranquillity of body and mind, turn aside selfish desires, and open the way to living more wisely, compassionately, and harmoniously with other humans, and with the natural environment, and with Sacred Reality. The use of experimental religious techniques slowly creates in the experimentor the religious characteristics which identify the follower of a religious path. As a convenience in discussing religious ways, I use the word "meditation" to refer to the initiatives taken by persons seeking to learn the skills that develop religious characteristics.

In the light of what I have accepted as dependable from my own Jewish-Greek-Christian traditions and from Asian religious traditions, I have concluded that following a religious way requires the practice of some form of meditation. Meditation seems to me to be the disciplined search for clearer understanding of what is true, good, and sacred, a search which includes experiments testing ways of living in harmony with the best that has been discovered. The results of such experiments should be constantly subject to re-examination, because it is apparent that people often err in their efforts to follow a religious path.

Sometimes, when I asked Asian friends how they happened to start along a religious way, they said they started with childlike curiosity, spontaneously, and then as they became more interested just continued along the path with many lapses in their diligence. Some said their motivation for taking initiative in using meditative techniques came from their awe as they became increasingly aware of the complexity, beauty, order and dependability in our ever-changing world. Others said they were moved to take initiative by a growing awareness of the ways people they admire (parents, relatives, teachers, friends) have contributed to what is seen as good and beautiful here on earth.

When I asked my Asian friends what initiative a follower of a religious path might take, I was told again and again that the safest and surest first step is to submit to a master, a guru, a teacher, because the skills needed for following a religious path are transmitted only person to person, "chest to chest." The guru, who imposes the disciplines needed for leading a life guided by true religious insights, will be honored and obeyed without question. Over the years, I have become increasingly uneasy with teachers who play the role of guru, expecting unquestioning obedience and admiration from their students; with gurus who enrich themselves through religious activities, who thrive on attention and popularity and power, who recruit disciples, who manipulate their followers. I am uneasy because of the harm done to students who become dependent, who accept without critical examination a guru's instructions (which sometimes have seemed to me to be seriously in error). And uneasy because of the harm done to the guru by servile adoration that encourages over-confidence and undue self-esteem, even on occasion, pious pride.

I have been most comfortable with religious seekers, whether teachers or students, who have found, with the *Tao-te-ching*, that the responsibility of the teacher is "to lead them, not to master them." Religious skills can be learned efficiently from teachers whose way of living and teaching is shaped by what they devoutly believe to be true; and who expect integrity, attentiveness, diligence, and independent initiative from their students. When capable teachers are not available, religious skills can still be developed through reading, through music and the arts, through discriminating observations of the results of human actions (including our own), and through disciplining oneself.

A first technique to develop is skill in becoming empty, tranquil, receptive—free from the heedlessness of multiple distractions and obsessive desires that are obstacles to devout awareness. Hsun Tzu, some 2200 years ago, said, ''Cause him who is seeking for the Way (Tao) to make his mind empty, and then he can receive it;...cause him who desires the right (Tao) to make his mind unperturbed; when his mind is unperturbed, he can arrive at truth''[22] Many other traditional writings (and modern commentators) emphasize the need to be at ease with the world and with oneself, the need to achieve tranquillity in order to bring one's desires, thoughts, and actions, into harmony with what is true and good, in order to apprehend the Sacred.

The skills that make tranquillity possible involve quieting the body and stilling the monkey-mind that flits from distraction to distraction. The personal initiatives recommended for meditation by many Asian teachers take for granted that mind and body are so intimately interrelated that to try to control them separately is artificial. Often, the skills taught are designed to increase awareness of the intimate interplay of one's mind and body, the aim is to become more supple in physical and mental activities in order to be able to react spontaneously in greater harmony within oneself, with others, with the natural world, and with the Sacred.

Asians from quite different traditions usually agree that quieting the body is aided by skillful control of what is eaten and of the ways the body is exercised and rested. They tell us that the body may be calmed by those who avoid consuming anything that stimulates desires or passions, or causes lethargy or reduces perception. Some warn against (or even forbid) onions, or garlic, or spices, or shellfish, or meat—or only certain meats. Most warn of the dangers of alcoholic beverages and mind-altering drugs, and of eating too much or too little. Gandhi told me that the eater takes on the characteristics of the animal or vegetable eaten. After having adjusted to many diets in ashrams and monasteries in various parts of Asia, and having listened to hours and hours of instruction on the foods required by religious disciplines, I have concluded that a diet balanced according to the best knowledge of the times is sufficient guidance for eating in ways that help to quiet the body and the mind. Food makes little difference to the follower of a religious path so long as it can be eaten without allergic reaction or revulsion or addiction or pride in one's asceticism, so long as it contributes to healthy energy, can be remembered for a day or two as adequate, pleasant in taste and appearance, and then forgotten.

Exercise is another skill used in preparation for meditation. Different traditions offer different programs, like hatha yoga in India or t'ai-chi ch'uan in China, as techniques to establish disciplined harmony of mind and body. We are told that skill in quieting the body comes more readily to those who regularly use exercises that involve relaxing, stretching, and rhythmic movements to make their muscles more supple and enduring, and their movements more graceful. Such exercises increase the ability to relax tense muscles, and get the amount of rest, diversion, and sleep the meditator needs. Care must be taken that exercising is not pushed to the point of fatigue, for fatigue is an obstacle to meditation.

In the Asian religious traditions, many different postures for meditation are recommended, or required. Some people prefer to be on the floor, in the lotus posture or kneeling; some use cushions and others disdain them; some, as in the mosque, prefer to stand and kneel. Some teachers insist that a perfectly straight back is critical, whatever the posture. My preference after many experiments is a chair with a reasonably straight back, with arms to support my arms; some chairs seem to require a cushion. Whatever the posture, the aim is to choose a position that can be maintained comfortably without distraction, discomfort, or fidgeting. The hands may be placed on the arms of a chair, on one's knees, in one's lap, or in any position that has special symbolic significance, so long as the hands are still and can be forgotten.

Having taken a position, the first effort is to check all of the body to release tensions, beginning with the feet and moving to the top of the head, with special attention to the jaw and the muscles around the eyes. At first, that process will probably have to be repeated again and again, and will require considerable attention; but with practice it will become a quick and almost automatic skill.

A meditator who can sit quietly at ease for as long as desired may still find that the act of breathing is obtrusive and distracting. Some forms of yoga and of Buddhist meditation put great emphasis on elaborate breathing techniques as preparation for meditation. Some insist on continued guidance under a guru because of the possibilities for harm from extreme shallow or deep breathing; both Swamis and Bhikkhus warned me that breath deprivation or excessive breath can lead to altered states of conciousness, even to hallucination, and can do bodily harm through raising or lowering the temperature excessively. I have not been convinced of religious value in elaborately detailed practices of breath control. My study and experience suggest that, if breathing gets in the way, it helps to breathe slowly, counting the normal breathing in and breathing out with a slow rhythm up to ten times, and then forget the breath by centering attention on the the object of meditation. Thus, the distractions of one's body are laid aside.

As skill in calming the body develops, it becomes more apparent that the mind is equally restless, crowded with the clamor of insistent thoughts jumping around like monkeys in a tree. But with disciplined effort we can learn to control our minds and open them to new imaginative perceptions—to turn our attention from worries, or pain, or fears, or shame, or desires, and instead turn it towards an intentionally selected interest. Just as it takes many months of effort to be able to relax each muscle, and to calm the racing of the blood when excited, and to control the rhythms of breathing, so it takes months, even years, of effort to learn how to put unbidden thoughts from the mind and to center attention on what might be true and good. But these efforts are basic for gaining religious insight—and for checking for one's possible errors in judging what is true, what is good.

Again and again, when I was discussing with Asian religious teachers the skills needed for meditation, they pointed out that although there is occasionally an unusual person who seems to have been born with the ability to control the body and the mind, most people need years of conscious and often discouraging efforts before they develop the tranquillity that makes continuing meditation and spontaneous religious actions possible. The daily lives of most humans, they say, give rise to desires and striving and regrets, with reactions of fear and anger, speculative imaginings, and tense, problem-solving struggles. Often the technique recommended for "scouring the mind"—emptying it of distractions—is the repetition of a word or words that interrupt the pressing mental activity and quiet the mind so it can be receptive and open to religious concerns. In some traditions the repeated word or words may be called a "mantra," using mantra in the psychological sense of a device for interrupting a train of thought, or for clearing the mind so thoughts might be directed toward religious insights.

When the aim is simply to "still the monkey-mind," to prepare for meditation, the repetition of syllables or words without connotations, inherently meaningless sounds, is more effective than the repetition of words or phrases that might stimulate thought or an emotional response. As an example, after some experimenting I have found that a count-down remembered from childish games provides a series of sounds effective for me when repeated softly to myself at the rate of about a syllable a second, with a pause at the commas: "EE-nee-MEE-nee-MY-nee-MOH, KRAK-a-FEE-nee-FY-nee-FOH, AH-pa-LOO-sha, POP-pa-TOO-sha, RIK-ee-STIK-ee, that-is-all." The rhythm and effectiveness of the repetition is enhanced by noting each syllable with a slight movement of the fingers of one hand back and forth from thumb to little finger. The number of syllables does not seem to matter so long as they have no meaningful associations. At first I experimented with five, then with ten, and found that I prefer a somewhat longer series for clearing the mind. When a racing mind keeps sleep away, such a set of syllables may be tested by relaxing physically as completely as possible, then repeating the series of sounds slowly to see how soon sleep comes.

After initial quieting down we see more clearly the nature of the interfering distractions that keep coming back. We observe that if we have been angry we cannot attain tranquillity, that we are diverted from religious seeking when we hate, when we crave recognition, appreciation, money, power, ecstacy, rewards—that is, when we have selfish desires. And we observe, conversely, that when our attention has been directed beyond our own concerns, when we have been compassionate and have been trying to achieve harmony in our natural and human environment, then we are much freer from interfering personal desires and regrets, then we have better control of our thoughts and can direct them to the religious search.

The Tibetan Thogs-med bzang-po hoped that:

> Withdrawing completely from things that excite us,
> Our mental disturbances slowly decline.
> And ridding our minds of directionless wandering,
> Attention on virtue will surely increase.[23]

As we try to develop skill in attaining tranquillity we find that we begin to ask ourselves what we should have avoided, how we should have acted in order to be able to meditate. We recognize that we cannot be tranquil after we have taken advantage of others or sought self-aggrandizement, that before we can meditate we must make restitution, or apologize, or otherwise try to make amends for some things we have done or have not done.

As I puzzled over what I was hearing from Asian teachers about the obstacles that must be overcome in order to meditate, I gained new appreciation for their assertion that preparation for meditation must include a diligent effort to live a good life. Most seekers, they said, learn from their family and respected religious leaders that a good life is a turning away from self-interest in an effort to act in ways that are considerate, honest, generous, and are compatible with the actions of the their ablest fellow pilgrims.

Hindu Swamis said students who want to learn how to meditate must first show that they are trying to live a good life—otherwise the obstacles their actions create will blind them to the instruction they would receive. In Islamic communities, the leaders respected as rightly-guided said the students who are able to learn how to follow the Straight Path show their commitment through their efforts to act in ways that are consistent with the teachings of the Qur'an. In many Buddhist communities, a good life (which is seen as a necessary accompaniment to meditation or worship) is shaped by the Precepts: not to kill, nor steal, nor commit sexual misconduct, nor lie, nor use intoxicating liquor or drugs; not to speak of others' shortcomings, nor to praise oneself and blame others, nor to begrudge giving generously, nor to be angry, nor to speak ill of the Buddha, the Dharma, or the Sangha. These actions are to be avoided because they make it almost impossible to quiet down, to attain the tranquillity needed for meditation.

It is a common observation among teachers of Asian religious ways that integrity and compassionate, caring acts are to be encouraged because they open the way to the recognition of what is true, good, and sacred. And many Asian religious teachers have taught that anger, hatred, violence, greed, and all forms of self-centeredness must be avoided because they create obstacles along a religious path.

Pilgrims who follow a religious path experimentally receive helpful guidance when they evaluate and reflect on what has been accepted and taught in different religious traditions as true. The skills recommended for developing the personal characteristics needed to walk along a religious path in closer harmony with what seems to be true and good, and with what is seen with wonder as Sacred, are tested experimentally and modified through experience again and again. What follows is a discussion of the roles reflective and devotional meditation play in experimental efforts to follow a religious path.

Six

Reflective Meditation

What is said here about meditation combines teachings I have found worthy of serious consideration, drawn from several Asian religious traditions. My selections are obviously biased by the notion that to follow a religious path is to take initiative in a search for insight into what is true and good and sacred, and to take responsibility for acting in harmony with the insights discovered. There are other religious paths not mentioned here: some distrust initiative, some find it unnecessary, some seem to me to be by-paths.

As tranquillity and openness develop in the religious seeker through the use of preparatory meditation skills, experiments in reflective meditation and in devotional meditation bring new insights to followers of a religious path. Reflective meditation helps the seeker see more clearly the realities—including the sacred—presented in human experience. Devotional meditation opens the way to a clearer awareness of Sacred Reality, and moves the seeker to act more effectively to increase the good in the world.

In reflective meditation, the aim is critical analysis

and evaluation of observations about what in the reality is seen as true, as good—and how to act in the light of the insights discovered. In reflective meditation, a seeker focuses the mind on a single religious insight seen as intriguing or important, and after careful, multifaceted consideration accepts or rejects—or modifies and then accepts—the insight as a true and good guide to human action.

Reflective meditation requires tranquillity of body and mind, and centering of attention on one insight at a time. Skill in reflective meditation slowly increases in those seekers who diligently make the effort to attain tranquillity and who learn how to focus their attention on chosen insights—thus avoiding what my Asian friends call the "monkey-mindedness" of flitting restlessly from this to that. At the outset, attention can be centered by repeating the insight or the question several times. If the mind wanders, attention may be forced back by returning to the repetition and then continuing the evaluation until the insight has been examined from many perspectives.

The insights examined in reflective meditation are chosen from the seeker's own observations, or may have been suggested by persons who are admired and trusted. They may be traditional observations or current speculations concerning what is true and good. Religious insights come to us through experience in the natural world and in human society, through oral instruction, through reading, and through the arts. The insights we choose to examine in reflective meditation may be illusions, may be partly in error, and may be true. In so far as time and circumstances permit, they are evaluated in meditation and tested in human experience.

The old Chinese proverb (really old, it was quoted by Hsun Tzu in the third century B.C.E.) is apt: "a short rope cannot draw water from a deep well." Reflective meditation is an attempt to lengthen our rope. Once the meditator reaches a decision about a topic, that topic becomes part of the background for future judgments; it will be re-examined in each later meditation to which it is relevant. Regular practice of reflective meditation develops the ability to keep attention focused as intended, to put aside distractions, to recognize some illusions, errors, and personal shortcomings. Thus, it gradually becomes possible to concentrate on insights that are increasingly complex—a sign that the short rope has been lengthened, that skill in using techniques for following a religious path has increased.

When in reflective meditation the followers of Asian religious paths consider the natural world, many of them perceive themselves simply as participants, along with all other forms of life, in a mysterious, constantly changing environment. When they reflect on their experience, they conclude that their role as humans is to adapt to the given regularities they have discovered in the natural world, to avoid as best they can the destructive changes in their environment, and to increase such good and beauty as seems to them to be possible in the circumstances. They often react to the natural world with grateful enjoyment, and with awe that hints at the presence of the sacred.

Their religious rituals indicate that their meditative reflections are sometimes centered on the ways plants and animals (including humans) on the earth are influenced by the sun, moon, planets, stars and lightning, winds, snow, rain, floods, volcanoes, and earthquakes. They may consider the power and sacred character of mountains such as Fuji or the Himalayas, and of lakes and rivers and oceans. They find some plants sacred (such as kusi grass, the lotus, the pine), and many plants necessary for all forms of life. Many animals are seen as having special religious significance: monkeys, elephants, cows, peacocks, snakes, foxes, for instance. The followers of Asian religious paths are often reminded of how intimately humans are involved in the natural world around them.

Reflective meditation is also concerned with the ways humans act and react to each other. We see selfishness, cruelty, indifference, violence, addiction giving rise to actions as dangerous and threatening as any from a typhoon or volcano. And we also see acts of spontaneous compassion, self-forgetting kindness, perceptive understanding, and beautiful creativity. Among the people of all the traditions of Asia—in whatever different physical, economic, and political circumstances—we observe efforts to reconcile conflicts, to help the sick and hungry, to care for orphans, to provide hospitals and schools. We see joy and gratitude expressed in festivals and rituals, and family gatherings. The realization that it is possible to choose and achieve such actions creates a sense of wonder that comes from reflective meditation on human actions in the natural world.

Reflective meditations on the given realities of the natural world and on human experience have stimulated developments in the natural and social sciences, and religious meditations have been greatly benefited by scientific discoveries. In their efforts to choose wisely, religious seekers have been aided for centuries by scientists who have contributed to human understanding of many of the given realities which are independent of conscious human choices, and of realities which are the result of human manipulation. The scientific explorations of our world from the smallest particle to the extremes of space, through the whole range of adaptations of living things in the sea, on land, and in the sky, provide insights into the realities now recognized by human consciousness. Scientists and religious meditators share curiosity about the realities humans experience. In the search for understanding they share a devotion to truth, integrity, open-mindedness, and ingenuity; a willingness to disclose how conclusions were reached, so they may be retested by others; and a willingness to modify any conclusion in the light of new discoveries.

Although some scientists end their search with the discovery of what is real, the religious awareness sought in reflective meditation is concerned both with what is true and what is good. The follower of a religious path seeks to know as much as possible about the nature of the world, and then must decide in the light of that knowledge what is possible and good to do. The religious seeker is aware, for instance, that the bronze which was first invented by devout artisans to express religious insights in enduring images was then used for destructive weapons in war; that medicines discovered to ease or cure suffering can be used as poisons. The goal of reflective meditation is to know what is good, and how to do it.

Reflections on our own observations of the natural world, of our fellow humans and ourselves, are always modified by what we have absorbed from other seeker's reflections that come to us orally, or in writings or works of art. Some religious leaders distrust personal observations concerning what is real and good, others judge such observations by their agreement with accepted religious writings, others allow individual initiative only as a last resort. Although most seekers turn to writings for guidance in meditation, some consider oral guidance essential, and some put their trust almost exclusively in the arts.

Reliance on the spoken word is chancy—for it requires that a seeker and the teacher who has some insight into what is true shall come together at the right time. Spoken words may be especially persuasive because of admiration for the person who speaks, or admiration for the way the words are presented, quite apart from the truth or falsity of the words. Even so, in each of the religious traditions of Asia they emphasize that person-to-person religious instruction is an effective way to transmit religious insights, that the comments of wise and good persons, the questions and clarifications shared by people of different experiences and insights, all contribute to growth in understanding and to strengthened resolves. They tell us that a perceptive person who has made some progress in developing the skills needed for following a religious path can often speak directly to the needs and concerns of seekers who are willing and able to listen. Through reflective meditation on spoken

138 / Reaching for the Moon

teachings, the seeker develops skill in listening attentively and selecting instructions worthy of serious consideration.

Writings concerning what is seen as true and good are the most widely used source of religious ideas examined in reflective meditation. They may be scriptures cherished as divine revelations, such as the *Vedas* or the *Qur'an*, or writings revered as inspired insights of superior persons whose guidance has been found trustworthy, such as the Buddhist Sutras or the *Bhagavad Gita* or the *Tao-te-ching*. For some, reflective meditation may begin with any writing judged to be a useful guide to religious understanding, whether it be scientific, historical, speculative, analytical, descriptive, or imaginative. Writings provide in an available form religious insights that have been treasured for many generations in many cultures, as well as new insights yet to be examined and tested. Writings have the advantage that they may be read and reread when the time is right for the meditator. The insights taught may be accepted or modified or laid aside at any time without embarrassment or affront to the author, or any obligation to point out errors or faults seen as biases in race, class, age, sex, or social organization. In meditation on religious writings from earlier times and other cultures, the recognition of human biases often leads to examination of biases in oneself.

In reflective meditation a written passage may be selected for careful examination: is it true? if true, what does it imply for actions that are good? Attention is centered on the passage as long as awareness and understanding seem to be growing. Sometimes the quotation leads to a new insight that makes a significant difference in one's understanding—then the reflective meditation continues with exploration of its possible implications for thought and actions. Sometimes a passage is laid aside as not relevant and later discovered to be far more significant than was seen at first; and sometimes a passage that has been highly recommended is laid aside and never considered for reflective meditation even after seeing it again and again.

The following passages from writings cherished in
several Asian traditions are examples of quotations recommended to me by Asian friends as selections they have found
worthy of careful examination in reflective meditation. In
these passages much of the emphasis is on the personal
characteristics needed in order to become skillful in the reflective meditation and the devotional meditation that
make it possible to follow a religious path.

Many Muslims have memorized large parts or all of
the *Qur'an*, making it readily available for reflective meditation. These passages have been quoted to me again and
again by Muslims from Morocco to Indonesia and Taiwan:

O all you who believe, seek you help
in patience and prayer; surely God is
with the patient.

•

Your God is One God;
there is no god but He,
the All-merciful, the All-compassionate.

•

Surely in the creation of the heavens and the earth and the
alternation of night and day and the ship that runs in the sea
with profit to men, and the water God sends down from heaven
therewith reviving the earth after it is dead and His scattering
abroad in it all manner of crawling thing, and the turning about
of the winds and the clouds compelled between heaven and
earth—surely there are signs for a people having understanding.

•

True piety is this:
to believe in God, and the Last Day,
the angels, the Book, and the Prophets,
to give of one's substance,however cherished,
to kinsmen, and orphans,
the needy, the traveller, beggars,
and to ransom the slave,
to perform the prayer, to pay the alms.
And they who fulfil their covenant
when they have engaged in a covenant,

and endure with fortitude
misfortune, hardship and peril,
these are they who are true to their faith,
these are the truly godfearing.[24]

Hindus have often recommended these passages
from the *Bhagavad Gita* for reflective meditation:

He who is not perturbed by adversity, who does not long for
happiness, who is free from attachment, fear, and wrath, is
called a muni of steady wisdom.

•

He who is not attached to anything, who neither rejoices nor is
vexed when he obtains good or evil—his wisdom is firmly
fixed.

•

The man of self-control, moving among objects with his senses
under restraint, and free from attachment and hate, attains
serenity of mind.

•

That man who lives completely free from desires, without
longing, devoid of the sense of "I" or "mine," attains peace.

•

Therefore always do without attachment the work you have to
do.

These, for Hindus, are characteristics of the follower
of a religious way:

Fearlessness, purity of heart, steadfastness in knowledge and
yoga; charity, self-control, and sacrifice; study of the
scriptures, austerity, and uprightness; non-violence [ahimsa],
truth, and freedom from anger; renunciation, tranquillity, and
aversion to slander; compassion to beings and freedom from
covetousness; gentleness, modesty, and absence of fickleness;
courage, forgiveness, and fortitude; purity, and freedom from
malice and overweening pride—these belong to him who is born
with divine treasures.[25]

For many centuries Buddhists have recommended
meditation on the Ten Perfections:

Liberality, Morality, Renunciation, Wisdom, Energy,
Forbearance, Truthfulness, Resolution, Good Will,
Equanimity.

And on the Eightfold Path, as presented in the Buddha's
first sermon:

Now this, monks, is the Noble Truth of the Path Leading to
the Cessation of Suffering: verily it is this Noble Eightfold
Path, namely, right understanding, right thought, right
speech, right action, right livelihood, right effort, right
mindfulness, and right concentration.[26]

Many Buddhists have set their standards for human
conduct after meditating on passages from the *Dhammapada:*

Overcome anger by loving-kindness, evil by good. Conquer
the niggardly with liberality, with truth the speaker of
falsehoods. . . . Speak the truth; give not way to anger, give of
your little to him that asks of you.

•

In those who harbor such thoughts: "He reviled me, he beat
me, he overpowered me, he robbed me," anger is never
stilled. . . . Hatred never ceases by hatred in this world.
Through loving-kindness it comes to an end. This is an ancient
Law.

•

Well done is that deed which, done, brings no regret; the fruit
whereof is received with delight and satisfaction.[27]

These excerpts have been taken from *The Thirty-Seven
Practices of All Buddhas' Sons*, by the Tibetan Bodhisattva
Thogs-med bzang-po, as examples of passages selected for
intensive reflective meditation, asking as usual the questions, Is it true? If so, what are the consequences?:

First listen, think hard, then do much meditation—
    The Sons of the Buddhas all practise this way. . . .
And ridding our mind of directionless wandering,
    Attention on virtue will surely increase. . . .
Turn from all actions that harm other beings. . . .
All of our sufferings, without an exception,

Derive from the wish to please but ourselves. . . .
Replace thoughts of self with concern for all others.
Thus when we conceive a compulsive attraction
    Toward whatever object our senses desire,
Abandon it quickly without hesitation. . . .
In short then, whatever we do in whatever
    Condition or circumstance we may confront
Should be done with the force of complete self-awareness
    Which comprehends fully the state of our mind.
Then always possessing alertness and memory,
    Which keep us in focus and ready to serve,
We must work for the welfare of all sentient beings—
    The Sons of the Buddhas all practise this way.[28]

Tzongkhapa, who died in Tibet in 1419, taught in
Steps of the Path:

Patience is defined as the state of mind in which you do
not become disturbed or upset by suffering or by those who
do harm. To perfect it does not mean that you no longer
have enemies, but rather that you never become angered,
discouraged, or reluctant to help. . . . You will live in harmony
with everyone.[29]

The writings of the Soto Zen Buddhist Master Dogen,
who died in 1253, stimulate reflective meditation after seven
centuries:

To do good for others in anticipation of their gratitude and
happiness would appear to be better than doing evil, but this is
not true goodness because you are still thinking of your own
self. The truly good man does things for others, even if now or
in the future they are in no way aware of it. How much better
must the attitude of the Zen monk be! In considering people,
do not differentiate between the intimate and the distant.
Resolve to help all equally. Determine in your mind to benefit
others, whether lay or clerical, without self-interest or profit,
and without caring whether people know or appreciate your
actions. Furthermore, do not let others know that you are
acting from this standpoint. . . . Just practice good, do good
for others, without thinking of making yourself known so that

you may gain reward. Really bring benefit to others, gaining nothing for yourself. This is the primary requisite for breaking free of attachments to the Self.[30]

From *The Analects of Confucius:*

> The Master said, Without Goodness a man
> Cannot for long endure adversity,
> Cannot for long enjoy prosperity.

•

> The Good Man rests content with Goodness; he that is merely wise pursues Goodness in the belief that it pays to do so.

•

> He whose heart is in the smallest degree set upon Goodness will dislike no one.

•

> Of Tzu-ch'an the Master said that in him were to be found four of the virtues that belong to the Way of the true gentleman. In his private conduct he was courteous, in serving his master he was punctilious, in providing for the needs of the people he gave them even more than their due; in exacting service from the people, he was just.[31]

Mencius, in the Confucian tradition in the 4th century B.C.E., tells us what he considers to be the qualities of a good person:

> It is by what he guards in his thoughts that the True Gentleman differs from other men. He guards Humanity and Propriety in his thoughts. The man of Humanity loves others. The man of propriety respects others. . . the True Gentleman simply does not worry.

•

> In the nurturing of the mind, there is no better method than that of cutting down the number of desires.

•

> A True Gentleman loves all living creatures.[32]

Mo Tzu, who probably taught after Confucius and before Mencius in the second half of the fifth century B.C.E., raised questions about human participation in war:

If someone kills one man, he is condemned as unrighteous
and must pay for his crime with his own life. According to this
reasoning, if someone kills ten men, then he is ten times as
unrighteous and should pay for his crime with ten lives, or if
he kills a hundred men he is a hundred times as unrighteous
and should pay for his crime with a hundred lives.

Now all the gentlemen in the world know enough to
condemn such crimes and brand them as unrighteous. And yet
when it comes to the even greater unrighteousness of offensive
warfare against other states, they do not know enough to
condemn it. On the contrary, they praise it and call it
righteous. . .

Now if there were a man who, on seeing a little bit of black
called it black, but on seeing a lot of black, called it white, we
would conclude that he could not tell the difference between
black and white. . . . Now when a great wrong is committed
and a state is attacked, men do not know enough to condemn
it, but on the contrary praise it and call it righteous.[33]

The *Tao-te-ching* has for centuries stimulated reflective meditation in China and Japan and Southeast Asia:

The best (man) is like water.
Water is good; it benefits all things and does not
    compete with them.
It dwells in (lowly) places that all disdain.
That is why it is so near to Tao.
(The best man) in his dwelling loves the earth.
In his heart, he loves what is profound.
In his associations, he loves humanity.
In his words, he loves faithfulness.
In government, he loves order.
In handling affairs, he loves competence.
In his activities, he loves timeliness,
It is because he does not compete
    that he is without reproach.
                        •
I treat those who are good with goodness,
And I also treat those who are not good with goodness.
Thus goodness is attained.
                        •

There is nothing softer and weaker than water,
And yet there is nothing better for attacking
hard and strong things.[34]

The writings that go under the name *Chuang Tzu*,
from about the fourth century B.C.E., provide many provocative passages and stories:

Heaven-based roamed on the south side of Mount Vast, and
came to the bank of the River Limpid. Happening to meet a
man without a name, he asked him, "Permit me to inquire
how one rules the Empire."
"Away! You're a bumpkin! What a dreary thing to talk
about! I am just in the course of becoming fellow man with the
maker of things; and when I get bored with that, I shall ride
out on the bird which fades into the sky beyond where the six
directions end, to travel the realm of Nothingwhatever and
settle in the wilds of the Boundless. What do you mean by
stirring up thoughts in my heart about such a trifle as ruling
the Empire?"
He repeated the question. Said the man without a name,
"Let your heart roam in the flavourless, blend your energies
with the featureless, in the spontaneity of your accord with
other things leave no room for selfishness, and the Empire will
be in order."

•

Virtue is the establishment of perfect harmony.[35]

Those passages are examples of writings that religious
seekers have for centuries evaluated in reflective meditation
and recommended as providing trustworthy guidance toward what some sensitive, discerning, reverent persons
have recognized as true and good.

Insights for reflective consideration also come from
other kinds of writings: philosophical and theological speculations, historical analyses, critical interpretations, and
imaginative parables, stories, dramas, and fantasies. For
instance, the *Jataka Tales* of the Buddha's previous existences have been influential in shaping the way Theravada
Buddhists see the realities of their world. The *Ramayana*

and the *Mahabharata* epics are cherished by Hindus as stories embodying traditional religious insights to be examined in reflective meditation. In China, *The Journey to the West* records the antics of the monkey Wu-k'ung in poetry and prose stories that make subtle provocative comments on Buddhist, Taoist, and Confucian religious teachings—comments often missed by contemporary readers who lack religious curiosity. Such imaginative stories about supernatural happenings have had wide influence on the thinking of Asians when they ponder the realities of their daily life.

Reflective meditation finds new insights in the verbal arts of story and drama, and also in works created by artists who prefer to express their religious insights through music, or dance, or painting, or sculpture, or architecture. Works of religious art are created by persons of unusual talents who express in ways that are most natural to them what they have discovered with wonder to be true and beautiful and sacred.

The religious seeker is asking: what does this work of art express about reality? about possible good in the world? about possible glimpses of the sacred? about ways of acting in harmony with the world we know through human experience? The artist's answers may sometimes be in error, either as to the insight or the mode of expression, but over the years many great works of religious art have brought to religious seekers insights into sacred reality that did not come any other way.

In reflective meditation the first step is to see or hear the work of art until it becomes familiar and can be readily recalled. In seeing, one remains quietly looking at the painting or sculpture, for instance, concentrating attention on what is seen, letting the imagination move freely but always coming back to what is being seen. The length of time will vary, and the observing will be repeated when possible until there is a sense of familiarity that makes recalling much easier, until reflection on what was discovered can be continued apart from the seeing. In hearing, as in seeing, the listener relaxes and concentrates attention on the sounds, letting the mind roam freely with the music but not wander away to other thoughts, and hearing the music again and again, so it becomes familiar. The religious seekers will observe the art and their reactions to it critically and appreciatively, and will continue to observe and decide to what extent the art object or the music communicates insights that are seen with reverence.

Sculpture, paintings, temples, mosques, caves, and gardens have the advantage—like books—that they can be seen repeatedly at the convenience of the seeker. They may be seen at different times, in different lights, from many angles, and sometimes can be known through photographs. As the details become fixed in memory after careful observation, they may be recalled again and again in reflective meditation.

The performing arts—like oral instructions—make difficulties for the meditator in two ways. Each performance is unique and ephemeral—we cannot return to it again and again to acquire familiarity. Moreover, the experience is intrinsically sequential, so that only one shifting moment of the unfolding whole is ever directly before us. Conversely, a performance has great strength in the excitement of unique and living confrontation, and in the learning that comes from being drawn progressively through imaginatively shaped experiences involving religious insights. Training of the memory clearly will play a role in successful meditation on performances of religious dance, drama, and music.

In recent years the religious arts (and oral teachings) have become more readily available for reflective meditation through recordings, tapes, film, slides, and video that can be seen and heard in public gatherings and in private, at different places and times. Increasingly, it is possible to have reproductions of religious arts as available as books, so they may be examined for religious insights worthy of serious consideration in reflective meditation. Although a great number of books dealing with the variety of religious beliefs and practices throughout the world have been published in this century, they must be translated into many languages if they are to be widely used for meditation. The reproductions of the religious arts, on the other hand, cross the language barriers without translation. The cultural barriers, also, are for many people more easily crossed by reproductions of religious arts and rituals than by translations of writings.

Nowadays religious seekers can develop skill in reflective meditation by first becoming physically and mentally more tranquil, then centering their attention on what seems to them to be good and sacred in their own experience and in religious insights presented by others in writings and works of art from many religious traditions. Clearly, choices must be made as to which of the techniques recommended for diligent and discriminating reflective meditation are most effective in recognizing trustworthy religious insights and in avoiding the absurd, the trivial, the irrelevant. With practice, some techniques make it easier to calm down and center one's attention and decide what can be accepted as true, and as good—and sometimes the techniques open the eyes of the seeker to a glimpse of the sacred.

Religious reflective meditation is a search for such dependable insights as humans can have about how to act in harmony with what is true and good. Asian religious teachings suggest that religious seekers must develop certain characteristics (such as tranquillity or compassion), and avoid certain other characteristics (such as anger or hatred), in order to be able to attain dependable understanding and the ability to act in closer harmony with the true and the good. Reflective meditation is first directed toward understanding what characteristics are needed in order to follow a religious path, and how they may be acquired. As those characteristics develop, the religious seeker gains new understanding of the given limits faced by all living humans; and of how intimately humans are involved in the natural world; and becomes more aware of the sacred power which is making good possible. As those characteristics develop, the religious seeker grows in awareness and understanding and thus can become more skillful in acting in ways that help possible good become actual. The quotations given above as examples for reflective meditation show something of the variety of characteristics recommended for all followers of a religious path. According to the passages quoted, a religious person becomes: serene, tranquil, self-controlled, steadfast, truthful, wise, energetic, generous, faithful, courteous, gentle, compassionate, merciful, non-violent. A religious person acts with loving-kindness, with self-awareness, works for the welfare of all sentient beings, with concern for all others, helps all people equally, loves humanity, loves all living creatures, treats everyone with goodness, chooses the right livelihood in order to live in harmony with everyone, and in the spontaneity of the accord with other things, leaves no room for selfishness.

Such lists of the characteristics needed in order to recognize the good, and to act in ways judged to be good, have been made for many centuries. In the fourth century B.C.E., Chuang Tzu gave us this list of the characteristics of the True Man of Old:

His figure looms but suffers no landslides:
He seems to lack but takes no gifts.
Assured! his stability, but not rigid:
Pervasive! his tenuous influence, but it is not on display.
Lighthearted! Seems to be doing as he pleases:
Under compulsion! Inevitable that he does it.
Impetuously! asserts in a manner of his own:
Cautiously! holds in the Power which is his own.
So tolerant! in his seeming worldliness:
So arrogant! in his refusal to be ruled.
Canny! Seems he likes to keep his mouth shut:
Scatterbrained! Forgets every word that he says.[36]

In this century, when I asked Asians how a person can follow a religious path, they usually started by listing the characteristics such a person needs and then told how those characteristics might be acquired and preserved. As a devout Hindu, Gandhi stressed courage and diligence (which he said he found in the second chapter of the *Gita*), and self-control, asceticism, ahimsa, devotion to truth, compassion, and devotion to God. Tagore stressed disciplined study and awareness of the natural world, of beauty observed in nature and created by humans, and of the needs of human societies. Some Hindus started their list with "lila" the spontaneous playfulness of the Gods, creating the beauty of the dance, of music, and the arts, and providing the means for humans to express their gratitude. Many Muslims listed the characteristics of Allah as characteristics expected of the Muslim, of one who submits, most frequently starting with compassion, mercy, forgiveness, and often emphasizing patience. Several times they said that for humans a common characteristic should be "adat," defined as gracious action in the circumstances, an act of courtesy, generosity, hospitality, of sensitive and uncalculating kindliness. Buddhists, who over the centuries have adapted their Buddhism to many different cultures, have chosen compassion and freedom from desires as the basic characteristics of followers of the path of the Buddha. The other personal characteristics they seek, or try to avoid, seem to be practical consequences of their compassion.

As I reflected on what I was learning from Asian religious teachings about the characteristics shaping the thoughts and actions of the followers of a religious path, I came to the conclusion that the *way* we think and act from day to day is the first concern for the religious seeker. We may not be able to control the end, but we can choose the means. Chuang Tzu wisely said, "The Way comes about as we walk it."[37] The characteristics of our thoughts and our actions may be all that we humans can control for sure, the outcome may be shaped by circumstances beyond our control. The results of our actions may be quite different from what we had expected, but the way we act is our choice, the characteristics of our actions are our own responsibility. The follower of a religious path chooses to act in ways that have the characteristics recognized as determining a religious way of life, to act in ways that are characteristically compassionate, caring, kindly, generous, honest, patient, and the like.

The characteristics we try to develop as we walk a religious path may vary with experience and understanding and circumstances. As of now, I am inclined to accept the judgment that anyone who chooses to follow a religious path will seek to act in ways that include as many of these characteristics as are fitting in the circumstances: *initiatives* such as diligence, curiosity, imaginative spontaneity, joyfulness, and playfulness; *awareness* which includes honesty, courtesy, patience, tranquillity; *consideration for others*, shown in love, compassion, caring, kindness, mercy, gentleness, generosity; and *reverence* expressed in wonder, awe, trust, and gratitude. Over the years I have known men and women who consider quite different religious characteristics to be essential—omitting some that seem to me to be important, and adding some I have omitted. Some pilgrims seem to walk their path spontaneously without conscious effort, but others go from day to day falling short, trying again and again. We hope that Rumi was right when he said, "A man comes to be the thing on which he is bent."[38] We recognize that the characteristics of our thoughts and actions determine the kind of person we become.

The same written and oral sources that give us such varied instructions about seeking religious characteristics also urge the seeker to be free from fear, anger, wrath, hate, malice, pride, regret, worry, compulsive attractions, desires, attachment, selfishness, sense of "I" or "mine," thinking of one's own self, pleasing oneself, seeking appreciation from others, disliking anyone, participating in offensive war, or even competing with others. Actions with those irreligious characteristics are insuperable obstacles to the religious way of life, we are told. In so far as those characteristics are tolerated, the religious way is neglected, even negated. For centuries, Hindus have taught that it is self-destructive to hate because it is an observable regularity of human experience that what we hate we imitate, the evils we fight we adopt. For an equally long time the Jains have pointed out that efforts to overcome evil tendencies by restraints have only temporary results. They taught that as religious seekers gain increasing skill in ahimsa, in acting with compassionate concern for others, their self-interest and its evil consequences wither away through neglect. This is ancient wisdom. The Jains made these observations some thousand years before the Sufi Rabi'a, who lived in the 8th century c.e., was asked, "Do you hate the Devil?" "My love of God," she replied, "leaves me no leisure to hate the Devil."³⁹

The list of things not to do poses a further problem: even if a person were to become free from all irreligious characteristics, such a person would only be avoiding some of the obstacles along the way, but could still lack any of the characteristics of a religious person. A stone is free from all the negative, defiling characteristics on this list. Time and energy spent in trying to be like a stone might be better spent in learning to act in ways that have religious characteristics, in developing, as Chuang Tzu suggested, the skills needed to act so that "in the spontaneity of your accord with other things," with what is true and good and sacred in the day by day realities of human experience, you "leave no room for selfishness." The irreligious characteristics are avoided through neglect when seekers give their full attention and energy to acting in ways that are open, honest, compassionately considerate of others, generous, patient; when followers of the path are reverently, gratefully aware of the good and the sacred in the world.

As I puzzled over the various lists of characteristics I found that the characteristics I was putting aside as irreligious were self-serving, and the characteristics I judged to be religious turn attention away from oneself.

When I reflected on the many men and women in Asia who patiently answered my questions and explained their religious beliefs and practices, I found myself wondering what made some of them seem to me unusually able, insightful, and, yes, inspiring in their presentation of their religious ideas. When I examined my reactions to the Asians whose teachings seemed to me to merit serious study, I recognized that I most admired men and women whose sympathetic concern was directed away from themselves to the world around them and to other human beings—men and women who, without thought of any possible personal advantage or of the impression they might be making, found it natural to reach out with wonder and gratitude for insights that would enable them to accomplish what appeared to them as good.

A Muslim friend, a devout scholar who was an able teacher and counselor, declared flatly that a religious path can only be one revealed by Allah and followed as Allah directs. A Zen master who was living joyfully the disciplined life of a monk, a sensitive, generous man who had little time to do anything other than serve his students and colleagues, would smile indulgently at the suggestion that there might be such a thing as revelation, and dismiss it as illusory. A kindly, wise, and gentle Vedantist in South India, who spent his life as a teacher of young people and was patient in introducing me to many of the intricacies of Hindu thought, was sure that the revelations received by the ancient rishis and then explained more recently by such teachers as Ramakrishna and Vivekananda were sufficient for all human beings. I knew these devout men well. I recognized that each of them perceived the world in quite different ways, and that there were significant variations in what they taught and what they did—and I admired them for their compassion and their unselfconscious efforts to act with increasing awareness of truth and goodness.

My friends sometimes suggest that I am forcing Asian religious beliefs and practices into a preconceived mold by saying I learned there that turning to concerns outside oneself is a requirement for following a religious path. I can say in defense only that I was not aware of beginning the study with such preconceptions, nor of having picked them up at Harvard University. On reflection, it seems to me that it was after I had begun the study of Asian religious ways through reading, observation, and conversations with Asian religious leaders that I gradually became aware that the religious search is a curious and compassionate turning to the world outside oneself. Somewhat reluctantly, I came to the realization that turning away from concern for one's own happiness, or recognition, or salvation, or even for doing one's duty, is a basic requirement for the religious way of life, a necessary step toward such insights into truth and goodness and the sacred as are possible.

At the outset I had been influenced by selective reading in the Bible in *Amos, Hosea, Isaiah, Psalms, Job,* the Sermon on the Mount, and Paul's chapter on love in *Corinthians,* and by such Christian devotional writings as *Theologia Germanica, Meister Eckhart,* and *Brother Lawrence.* Then my understanding of those writings was enlarged by many Asian writings, such as those recommended above for reflective meditation, stressing the need to turn away from selfish concerns. One of the many ways Sufis say it is illustrated in this passage from Rumi:

> Do you know a name without a thing answering to it?
> Have you ever plucked a rose from R,O,S,E?
> You name His name; go, seek the reality named by it!
> Look for the moon in the sky, not in the water!
> If you desire to rise above mere names and letters,
> Make yourself free from self at one stroke.[40]

The *Bhagavad Gita* says:

> He who is not perturbed in mind by adversity and who has no
> eagerness amidst prosperity, he from whom desire, fear and

anger have fallen away—he is called a sage of firm understanding. He who has no attachments on any side, and who does not rejoice nor hate when he obtains good or evil—his wisdom is firmly set.[41]

From the *Tao-te-ching*:

Therefore the sage acts, but does not rely on his own ability. He accomplishes his task, but does not claim credit for it. He has no desire to display his excellence.[42]

Zenkei Shibayama, a contemporary Zen Master, tells this old Zen story about Hyakujo, a distinguished Roshi who died in 814:

One day Hyakujo was walking with his teacher Baso. Seeing a wild goose flying in the sky, Baso asked Hyakujo, "What is it?" "A wild goose, Master," replied Hyakujo. Baso asked, "Where is it flying to?" Hyakujo replied, "It is already gone." Thereupon Baso clutched Hyakujo's nose and wrenched it. Hyakujo cried in pain. Baso demanded, "Do you say that it has flown away?" This at once awakened Hyakujo.[43]

When I reflect on what I have learned from followers of Asian religious paths, I see more clearly that the wild goose does not fly away from me, that I am not the center of what is happening, that the follower of a religious path is only a conscious part for a limited time of a wonderful, mysterious series of happenings in which humans participate.

These reflections have led to the conclusion that the obstacle of selfishness drops away as the follower of a religious path concentrates on developing the characteristics needed for living in harmony with the circumstances of day by day existence, for realizing such good as is possible, and for becoming more aware of the Sacred.

Reflective religious meditation leads to self-examination. After reflecting on what can be accepted as true about the realities humans discover through experience, and about the characteristics of human reactions that contribute to possible good in the world, those who are seeking religious insight ask: was that act kind? patient? was I aware of the other's needs and of my own shortcomings? have I treated those who are not good with goodness? how can I turn away from my self-centeredness? have I acted in such accord with the world that there was no room for selfishness? have I been growing in skill in acting with compassion, ahimsa, wu-wei? have I increased my awareness of what is true, good, of what some people see as Sacred Reality?

Many Asians have pointed out that frequent self-examination is a necessary technique for the religious seeker—self-examination which is an objective evaluation of the level of one's religious competence, one's adhikara, as the Swami taught me at Kalighat. Thich Tri Quang, as we have seen, said the first step along the religious way is to sit quietly and recall everything that one did the day before—such self-examination will always lead to shame for something that was done or was not done, and from shame comes a desire to do good, to do better this day. Recollection, Tri Quang said turns one away from self-centeredness toward the good. Gandhi urged that everyone should keep a daily journal, a recording of one's thoughts and actions that becomes a daily self-examination stimulating a desire to do better.

Kao P'an-lung, a Neo-Confucian scholar who died in 1626, stressed the need for self-examination. His ideal is a Sage, a person whose characteristics include attentiveness, awareness, activity, diligence, reverence, spontaneity, intimate relations with natural surroundings, freedom from selfishness and attachments. He said that the self-examination which makes those characteristics possible starts by sitting in a quiet place where the "stillness results in worldly delusions dispersing and melting away." Then, he said, the mind must be centered on the hard work of learning, for if "one leaves everything to spontaneity nothing will get done, no change or transformation will be accomplished and there will not even be any spontaneity." He recalled that one respected teacher said, "When we have even a single thought in our minds of criticism or fame, then our minds are still in the path of the small man," and this caused him to examine himself deeply. He said his teacher admonished, "All ridicule by family, state or the entire world must be disregarded. Do not be weak or timid!"[44]

Reflective self-examination of the characteristics of our own actions makes it possible to become more skillful in recognizing and lessening our anger, dislikes, self-indulgence, self-serving actions that ignore or even exploit other people; our despair, depression, self-condemnation; our pride, self-congratulation, condescension, indifference, neglect. When we see that we have acted in ways that are alien to religious characteristics, we often tend to become discouraged and to avoid continuing meditation. The best technique in such circumstances is to face and admit our shortcoming, and to make restitution where possible. Then to forget it and start fresh; start again trying to make sure the characteristics of our actions are religious.

Reflective self-examination of the characteristics of our actions increases our awareness of how to act more wisely, patiently, compassionately; how to be more considerate of the feelings and motivations of others, and to contribute to the common welfare. The growing awareness of how the religious characteristics enhance the good helps to turn a religious seeker away from self-centeredness. It is a humbling discovery of reflective self-examination that resolution and commitment are only a first step, that efforts to act with compassionate concern must be renewed, tested, and revised in the light of our best judgment as long as life continues.

A primary caution about self-examination—whether we note improvement or backsliding—is to avoid self-fascination or self-satisfaction. Sometimes, religious seekers who are experimenting with self-examination need to be reminded of E.B. White's theater critic who "scarcely saw the play at all for watching his reactions to it."

In reflective meditation, as we have seen, religious seekers study and observe religious insights with as much objectivity and skill as their cultural background permits; they make judgments as to what they consider to be true and good, and subject themselves to careful self-examination in the light of those evaluations. There often comes a time in reflective meditation when the follower of a religious path realizes that there is more to a religious way of life than simple agreement with the best religious ideas that have happened to come to their attention. Along the way, after learning as much as possible about the given realities faced by humans, and after self-examination in the light of the perceived realities, the next step for the religious pilgrim is to devotional meditation. Devotional meditation is a sincere effort to think and act in ways that are in harmony with what is seen as true and good and sacred—to move from agreeing to being, from good intentions to spontaneous good initiatives.

Seven

Devotional Meditation

Devotional meditation grows out of the awe and gratitude that comes from a haunting, difficult-to-express sense of the sacredness of an event, or place, or person—an awareness of the sacred that moves religious seekers from reflective observation and evaluation to devotional participation.

For followers of a religious path, the sense of the sacred comes from their awe and gratitude as they become aware of the changes in the complex realities of human existence: aware of dependable regularities in the natural world, such as the movements of sun and moon and stars and clouds, with season following season bringing changes in the rivers, lakes, oceans, mountains, plains, and all living things; aware of the amazing adaptability of all plants and animals to changing circumstances; aware of human birth, maturity and increasing knowledge; aware of the good and the beautiful, of friendship, love, generosity, joy and death. Followers of many traditions tell us that back of all the processes observed in human experience is the Sacred Reality which is moving toward such good as is possible in the world. Sacred Reality is given many names, and is knowable through human insights insofar as humans discover from day to day, and cherish, what is true, and good, and beautiful.

Devotional meditation opens the way to clearer awareness of sacred aspects of human experience when selected events, persons, and places are seen with wonder and thankfulness. As awareness of the sacred increases, self-centered concerns drop away, making it possible to become more skillful in the slow and difficult process of learning to act more consistently in self-forgetting spontaneous harmony with what is seen as Sacred Reality.

The skills developed through devotional meditation come through dedicated efforts continuing in spite of discouragement and failures, for the rest of one's life. It has also been noted that, like Walpole's three traveling princes of Serendip, followers of a devotional path will often chance upon wonders they did not know, nor seek. One of the given realities of human experience is that serendipity adds zest and keeps many a weary seeker going along the seemingly endless paths of science, reason, artistic creativity, and religious devotion.

People may turn to personal devotions from overflowing feelings of admiration, joy, and gratitude coming from their encounter with the wonders of human existence; or because they seek to develop more sensitive awareness, patience, and compassion. Some may turn to devotional meditation from a sense of their own weakness and need for help to break away from despair, or shame, or sorrow— or from what they sometimes call an agonizing sense of "dryness." Occasionally we discover a rare person who spontaneously follows a religious path, but most people find that in order to turn from their self-centered concerns they need the help of devotional meditation to acquire skills in thinking and acting that open the way to greater awareness of the sacred.

As awareness of the sacred increases, it becomes apparent in reflective meditation that even though many people have offered their lives and many have been killed for what they believed to be sacred, there may be errors in judging what is sacred. When self-centeredness has not yet dropped away, what has been called sacred may turn out to be trivial, may refer only to whatever is remembered with a comfortable feeling of self-satisfaction. It may be called sacred because it is unusual, or because it is a practice or belief of admired persons in a religious or social or national group with which one is identified. Devotional meditation, which leads to commitment to what is seen as sacred, needs reflective meditation for guidance.

Devotional meditation is experimental seeking for clearer awareness of the Sacred through self-forgetting acts of worship. Acts of worship are recollection (which includes study and observation and pilgrimage as modes of worship), prayer, and acts of compassionate caring for others. Caring acts have the religious characteristics (including freedom from self-centered concerns) that make it possible to live in closer harmony with what is seen as true and good and beautiful in the circumstances, and with what what is seen as Sacred Reality, what some pilgrims call God.

Communication between a religious seeker and Sacred Reality takes place in worship. In worship, those who turn warmly and openly to the world often have a sense of being in the presence of an Awareness that is more than an extension of our human awareness, a sense of being known as well as knowing, a sense of acquiring wisdom that is part of a greater wisdom. My Asian friends tell of a mystery not fully grasped, a mystery that is more than just a recognition of human ignorance, a Reality that experience proves to be trustworthy and to some extent knowable. The followers of a religious way of life tell us that the Reality in which we find ourselves is dependable, just and consistent, compassionate, loving, kind, forgiving, beautiful. Those who refer to any aspect of the realities of human existence as God, as Sacred Reality, see those qualities as divine char-

162 / *Reaching for the Moon*

acteristics permeating what we perceive, as characteristics of a given Reality that is knowable as a guide, a guardian, a forgiving and forgetting source of support. When, through worship, those religious characteristics become the characteristics of human actions, it is then possible for humans to discern what is good, and to act in self-forgetting harmony with the world as it can be known through human understanding.

Many followers of Asian religious paths have recommended techniques of worship to be used regularly either alone or with other followers of their chosen way. A highly respected Hindu scholar in Bombay recommended participating in traditional rituals as the first step toward gaining these skills needed to go on your own way. A Swami in Madras, on the contrary, insisted that initial religious practice must be alone, after instruction by a guru, with group participation growing out of insights tested in private. Gandhi, who assumed that any religious person would regularly take time for private devotions, found that he and the staff at his political headquarters needed a period of group worship every day, complete with scripture reading, prayer, chanting, and singing, drawn fram Hindu, Muslim, and Christian sources. For Allamah Tabataba'i, the respected traditional Shi'i scholar, dependable techniques for worship whether private or public are taught by the gnostic, "the one who worships God through knowledge and because of love for Him, not in hope of reward or fear of punishment." He cites the sixth Iman, "There are three kinds of worship: a group worship God in fear and that is the worship of slaves; a group worship God in order to receive rewards and that is the worship of mercenaries; and a group worship God because of their love and devotion to Him and that is the worship of free men. That is the best form of worship."[45]

The choice between private or group devotions seems to be a matter of preference. Again and again, when I was trying to learn why my Asian friends participated in public worship, they were surprised that I should ask. When pressed, some said they join in group worship to preserve traditions that are needed for an orderly society, or to carry on family customs; that group worship helps them live more harmoniously with their family and community. Some said that joining with others in worship strengthens their resolve to follow the religious way, and helps them see that way more clearly. Even when they judged some aspects of public worship to be trivial, or misguided, or selfish attempts by leaders to manipulate their followers, many devout seekers regularly participated in other group devotions they could trust because they found their awareness increased through being in a sacred environment, or through hearing sacred music, or through observing and joining with the devotions of their fellow worshipers. In group worship they are encouraged, they learn from each other, they are edged away from personal eccentricities to broader perspectives. Most of them said that the techniques of devotional meditation used in private devotions are also used in group worship, and skill in using such techniques is increased by using them both alone and with others.

It is often difficult to become alert to the presence of the Sacred, to lay aside our workaday distractions. Most of us are so involved in daily routines and established habits that to develop new ways of thinking and acting we need the help of frequent recollection of the inspiring religious insights we have found in religious writings or oral teachings, in music and the other arts, or in our direct experience of the beauty and variety and complexity of natural phenomena. As in learning a musical skill, we have to concentrate on and practice a new religious skill again and again, to ingrain the sought-after characteristics as unselfconscious normal patterns of action.

Recollection in devotional meditation, whether private or with others, may be study as a mode of worship, a devotional re-reading of a sacred writing as an accepted guide to intentions, and actions. It may be listening as a

mode of worship, listening again to familiar instruction
from respected teachers or to discussions with fellow seekers, or listening to familiar music that strengthens commitment to a religious way of thinking and acting. It may, as
an act of devotion, be observing familiar dance or drama,
or religious paintings, sculpture, or architecture. For those
with talents for creating poetry or music or works of art,
such creativity as a mode of worship may be recollection in
devotional meditation.

Sometimes, devotional meditation is recollection of
passages examined in reflective meditation (such as those
quoted above) and judged to be worthy of serious consideration for adoption as guides for one's own thoughts and
actions. The Shi'i business man in southern India reads Ali's
familiar writings again and again so that in the warm glow
from Ali's words he can remember to loose from himself
"the cause of every animosity" and return to work in harmony with himself and the people around him. His Hindu
neighbor starts the day reminded again that the *Gita* says,
"Therefore always do without attachment the work you
have to do." In Sri Lanka a Theravada Buddhist resolves to
remember to "speak the truth" and to "overcome anger
by loving-kindness." Muslims from Morocco to Indonesia
remind themselves, "Surely God is with the patient." In
China, an admirer of Confucius (who might be surprised to
be called a follower of a religious path) recollects that anyone whose heart is in the smallest degree set upon goodness
will love all living creatures. A Japanese Buddhist starts the
day quietly contemplating a picture of Bodhidharma cross-
ing a river on a single rice straw, and resolves that day to
try to be so light in the world that one straw would provide
all the support needed. A Buddhist neighbor recollects
again the resolve to benefit others, as Dogen taught,
"without caring whether people know or appreciate" what
is done, and to end the day able to say, with Rinzai, "there
is nothing I dislike."

Recollection in devotional meditation is strengthened

by repetition as a reminder of religious insights accepted but not yet fully realized in oneself. It may be repetition of the name of a God, or of a revered person, or of a sacred writing; or it might be a prayer, or a mantra, or a passage from a sacred writing, or a characteristic of Sacred Reality.

The repetition in Hinduism might be a mantra such as OM, or any of the 108 names of God, choosing the name associated with the characteristic most appropriate in the circumstances. Among Hindu bhaktis the emphasis is on awareness, loving, compassion, or on the Companion, the Sustainer. When Hindus follow the way of knowledge, the chosen characteristics will be those of the Knower revealing a dependable and sustaining world in which individuals can attain tranquillity and understanding. Hindus whose religious search follows the way of action see the God as generous, beneficent, a Bestower and Guide.

In Islam, there is the repetition of the five daily prayers, and the repetition of the 99 names of Allah revealed in the *Qur'an*. The Sufis favor remembrance of God by the repetition of the name of God or of a phrase that brings God to mind, that increases awareness of the presence of God, that is a reminder of God's characteristics. Some Muslim friends tell us that above all else, God is patient, and when we have discovered the divine patience all the rest that can be known about God and the characteristics of a Muslim—one who submits to God—follows. Other Muslims start with compassion, or with mercy, or forgiveness as the most important characteristic of God, and therefore for humanity. Frequently mentioned characteristics are generosity, justice, love, compassion, mercy, forgiveness.

Among Buddhists, passages from the Tipitakas or the Sutras may be repeated over and over in meditation. In Japan, Nichiren Buddhists recite *"Namu Myoho-renge-kyo,"* and millions of followers of Shinshu recite *"Namu Amida Butsu."* Tibetans repeat *"Om Mani Padme Hum"* as their powerful words that open the way to religious insights.

These are but a few examples of words and phrases repeated daily throughout Asia by followers of religious paths for whom a day without such repetitions is incomplete.

In my conversations with followers of religious paths in Asia, many of them said the regular repetition of their chosen phrases or names is a practice they must maintain in order to be increasingly aware of, and to communicate with Sacred Reality. For some, the repetition of words or names is a psychological technique for clearing the mind of distractions and maintaining tranquillity. For others, the repetition may serve that useful purpose as a first step and then is a devotional technique for centering the mind on religious teachings pointing to the Sacred, and for preparing to communicate with Sacred Reality through prayer.

The times for recollection and repetition may be left to the inclination of the devotee, or may be set by custom or by the authority of the religious group: daily, weekly, fortnightly, monthly, annually; times of birth, naming, maturing, marriage, and death; anniversaries of persons and events in the traditions of the religious community. Holy days may become major festivals serving as occasions for recollection and worship. Set times for religious reminders are often needed to help overcome the distractions and impediments that beset followers of a religious path. They provide occasions for reaffirmation of commitment and, as such, can generate energy and initiative for carrying out intentions. With practice at turning one's consciousness to the Sacred, what first needed laborious discipline can become natural and spontaneous.

The places for devotional meditation may be wherever the devotee chooses, preferably a building set aside as sacred such as a temple or mosque or ashram, or a sacred place where a religious event happened, or where an admired person lived—or maybe a garden, grove, cave, lake, river, or mountain cherished as holy. A place seen as sacred is a powerful reminder of religious insights associated with that place, and is an inspiring environment for devotional meditation.

Times and places recognized as sacred have given rise in Asian religious traditions to pilgrimage as a favored technique of recollection and worship for myriads of people. Pilgrims give many reasons for their pilgrimage. For some, pilgrimage is a search under the most favorable circumstances imaginable—at a sacred place at a sacred time—for clearer awareness of Sacred Reality and for the ability to act more wisely and compassionately. A pilgrimage may be undertaken as an act of repentance, seeking forgiveness; it may be an expression of sorrow after a death, or of gratitude for blessings received. Some pilgrims are fulfilling a ritual obligation or a vow, or seeking a particular blessing such as health or peace, or are hoping to attain merit. Some seem to have chosen the devotional technique of pilgrimage out of curiosity and the anticipated pleasure of traveling to a beautiful and quiet spot with like-minded people. And sometimes there are pilgrims who simply appear to be tourists enjoying a holiday.

The many pilgrimage places in Asia, well-known and obscure, are reminders of the importance of devotional meditation in the daily life of Muslims, Hindus, Buddhists, and followers of other paths. In Islam, it is well-known that pilgrimage to Makkah is required of every Muslim who is able to make the trip, and the experience is treasured as sacred. In Morocco I was told that several pilgrimages to Fes, or to Kairouan in Tunisia, would be as good as one to Makkah, or that having been to Makkah the other pilgrimages are equal to a second one to Makkah. When I was asking devout Shi'is about pilgrimages they always spoke highly of the pilgrimage to Makkah and had been there or hoped to go sometime, and then spoke warmly of their pilgrimages to Najaf and to Karbala in Iraq, the places made specially sacred for them by Shi'i Imams and events in Shi'i history. Once in Baghdad I was taken to a shrine for a Pir, a founder of a Sufi order, by a descendant who owned and cared for the shrine. There was a constant flow of devout pilgrims, praying and leaving gifts (which he, as owner, was free to dispense as he saw fit). In Indonesia, at Demak, I was told that when the Makkah hajj is not possible, four pilgrimages to Demak are equal to one to Makkah.

For Buddhists, Bodh Gaya, in central India, is the sacred place where the Buddha attained enlightenment at a spot where even today there is a bodhi tree. In the twentieth century small temples and hostels have been built there for pilgrims from many Buddhist countries. It has become a special place for Tibetans because the Dalai Lama comes once a year and recently gave the Kalachakra initiation there before tens of thousands of Tibetan refugees who are not able to go on pilgrimage to Lhasa, the Dalai Lama's rightful home. Sarnath, near Varanasi, where the Buddha preached his first sermon setting in motion the Wheel of the Dharma, has also become more popular as a pilgrimage center in this century as it has become easier to travel from distant countries. The Buddhists of Sri Lanka built a new temple there, with murals by a Japanese artist, and now hostels and shrines of several Buddhist traditions welcome pilgrims from abroad. In Burma, the Shwedagon pagoda was once described to me by a Theravada Buddhist as the ideal place for worship because the vibrations there are the best in the world for devotional meditation. In China, through all the political changes of recent years, Wutai and Tiantai have continued to be popular pilgrimage centers for followers of Mahayana Buddhist traditions. And in Japan several beautiful Buddhist temples at Nara and Kyoto, and Shinto shrines at Ise, are sacred places for worship for tens of thousands of pilgrims every year.

In India there are hundreds of sacred pilgrimage places, and for most Hindus a religious path includes pilgrimages, sometimes for short distances and sometimes arduous journeys to far away sacred shrines. A friend of mine, overcome with grief at the death of a relative, went on pilgrimage from southern India to Badarinath in the Himalayas and returned at peace with the world. At Hardwar, pilgrims told me that after bathing in the Ganges there they had no further need for temples or rituals, their religious search was complete. A business man in Bombay told me that the water of the Ganges he brought from Hardwar was treasured and used as medicine that protected his family from illness and evil. A professor in a university in central India said that the water of the Ganges purifies him of all evil thoughts or actions, intentional or inadvertent. Varanasi is sacred because of many events that happened there, and as a place to die, and as a place to perform ceremonies in memory of one's ancestors. The great mela at Allahabad, when hundreds of thousands of Hindu worshipers gather where the sacred Jumna and Ganges rivers join, is a particularly effective place and time for petitions and expressions of gratitude. A friend who had returned from study in the United States, went to the shrine at Tirupati to be purified so he could participate again in marriage and death ceremonies. Pilgrimages to Hardwar or Badarinath in the north, to Rameswaram or Cape Comorin in the south, to Kalighat or Puri in the east, and to Dwarka or Nasik in the west, may be undertaken for many reasons, and have the added merit of giving the pilgrim who worships there a sense of being identified with the centuries old religious traditions and aspirations of millions of ancestors in all of India.

When I asked followers of different religious paths of Asia how they gained increasing confidence in their awareness of the Sacred, they often described pilgrimage experiences as the occasions when new religious insights came to them.

Devotional recollections of traditional insights, observations, and pilgrimages bring a growing awareness of the sacredness of certain events, persons, and places. That awareness gives rise to a yearning toward the good, the Sacred—a yearning expressed through prayer and through experimental attempts to think and act in ways that are in harmony with what is judged to be Sacred Reality.

Prayer is an expression of aspiration, of hope, of longing. It is a conscious effort to communicate to Sacred Reality a human aspiration for greater awareness of the good, a hope that such good as is possible now may become actual, a longing for the ability to act in closer harmony with the good and thus with Sacred Reality. The communication may be expressed through words, or through the arts, or through unselfish acts, and always with the possibility that it will be received.

Prayer is addressed to a Sacred Reality that may be seen as personal or as impersonal, that may be called by many names and described in many ways, and is always revered as a reality superior to the person who prays. Human aspirations are communicated from the perspective of a lesser understanding, lesser ability, lesser goodness. The seeker turns to prayer out of the realization that alone, or even with the encouragement of like-minded seekers, more help is sought in order to turn consistently toward the good.

Prayers are involved in all the skills needed in devotional meditation: in the initial efforts to relax, and in devout recollection of traditional religious insights, and observations, and pilgrimages. The seeker who is experimenting with prayer may start by reciting traditional prayers and then try to construct prayers that are fitting for the circumstances, whether spoken or unspoken, a gesture, a work of art, a bodily posture, an act. Prayers may come spontaneously from feelings of awe, joy, gratitude, reverence, aspiration, regret, repentance, despair, compassion, love.

Many kinds of prayer are recommended for serious consideration. For some seekers, prayer is simply listening, sitting quietly as free as possible from distractions, waiting with a sense of being open to the holy, accepting what is "heard" and examining it critically for possible self-deception. The prayer of gratitude is a spontaneous expression of thankfulness for the experience of wonders and joys greater than humans can achieve for themselves. Reflective and devotional meditation give rise to the prayer of aspiration for the self-forgetting characteristics of the person who seeks the good, such as sensitive awareness, patience, compassion, love. Aspiration leads to the prayer of supplication for courage and perseverance and skill to be able to repent and make amends for past insensitivity and failures. When illness or accidental injury or cruelty or indifference bring depression or despair, the prayer of supplication is for ability to recognize the unchangeable and to bring all actions more in harmony with what is perceived as holy, true, good. Again and again the supplication is for clearer insight and the ability to act wisely and compassionately, free from selfish concerns. Intercessory prayers for another person or persons or community are, like personal prayers, spontaneous expressions of gratitude, aspiration, and supplication.

Seekers who have discovered that self interest is an obstacle along the religious path find it difficult to pray for selfish advantage for themselves, or others, or a nation—or to use prayer as a means to remind or to manipulate Sacred Reality, or any hearers who might be present.

The results of prayer, according to many devout seekers who follow Asian paths, are insights and resolves that are often worthy of careful consideration and experimental testing. People who have prayed in the ways discussed here report a sense of having spoken honestly, and of having been heard. Sometimes they have a sense of a burden of regret having been lifted, and often a sense of greater clearness of understanding and commitment. They describe an awareness of being in the presence of, and in closer harmony with, a Reality that is holy, a power greater than they have discovered in humans, either individuals, or groups, or nations, or all humanity.

In this discussion of meditation as a way of following a religious path, it has been suggested that seekers who choose to walk along a religious way take initiative by trying to develop the skills that bring tranquillity, and the skills of reflection and self-examination, and the devotional skills of worship, recollection, pilgrimage, and prayer. As skill in devotional meditation develops, one more devotional skill is needed: skill in acting in ways that have the religious characteristics that are in harmony with what has been seen as Sacred Reality—the Sacred Reality that is moving toward such good as is possible at a given place and time. Caring acts, acts that have religious characteristics, grow spontaneously out of sensitive awareness gained through reflective and devotional meditation that helps us to see ourselves in clearer perspective and turns our attention beyond ourselves to the good for other persons and for the world around us. In devotional meditation, acts that are characteristically compassionate, kind, patient, considerate, and the like, are acts of worship along with recollection, pilgrimage, and prayer.

Once, in Damascus years ago, when I was strolling along the street called Straight—wondering whether it is truly the most ancient street in the world that has served without interruption as a market place—I watched as a man who was riding slowly through the crowd on a bicycle with a basket of oranges precariously balanced on the handlebars was bumped by a porter so bent by a heavy burden that he had not seen him. The burden was dropped, the oranges were scattered, and a bitter altercation broke out between the two men, surrounded by a tight circle of onlookers. After an angry exchange of shouted insults, as the bicyclist moved toward the porter with a clenched fist, a tattered little man slipped from the crowd, took the raised fist in his hands and kissed it. A murmur of approval ran through the watchers, the antagonists relaxed, then people began picking up the oranges and the little man drifted away. I have remembered that as a caring act, an act of devotion there on the street called Straight by a man who might have been a Syrian Muslim, or a Syrian Jew, or a Syrian Christian.

Caring acts may be spontaneous reactions growing out of reflective and devotional meditation, they may be expressions of gratitude for the good we have recognized and experienced, they may also be experiments checking which of the so-called religious characteristics we can trust as being truly in harmony with the Sacred. As experimental, they are tests of the truth of religious insights accepted from scriptures, from teachers, from religious traditions, and from observing attempts to put those insights into practice. Caring acts test the validity of theological and philosophical speculations, test ahimsa and wu-wei, and may lead to alterations in insights that had been accepted as true. Even though some experiments may fail, may be discouraging, may cause regret and remorse, many insights tested by caring acts have proved to be dependable for followers of a religious path.

Seekers who have shown increasing skill in acting with caring awareness and concern find that through such acts their self-interest lessens and their understanding of what is good increases. With that understanding they realize that they are free to choose how they will react to whatever happens, and therefore are responsible for the characteristics of every reaction in thought and deed. Those who follow experimentally a religious path that turns away from selfish advantage discover that efforts to act with compassionate concern must be repeated and re-examined and reinforced as long as life continues. They discover that individual skills vary, and that all religious skills, even when they seem to be spontaneous, must be tested and revised in the light of such good judgment as comes from reflective and devotional meditation, and then must be checked by experiments using methods that have the characteristics of religious acts.

The caring follower of a religious path is inevitably involved in social concerns by the discovery of people harmed by illness, or accident, or neglect, or indifference, or lethargy, or ignorance, or condescension, or exploitation, or cruelty, or violence—and is moved by compassionate concern to help them. Growing awareness of those social concerns moves religiously caring followers to work for peace and harmony between and within groups, for rehabilitation of criminals, for health care, food, housing, and education for all. Persons who care try to protect our natural environment from destruction, and act in ways that lessen the prejudices against people who are scorned because they are different: because they are young, or old, a woman or a man, or happen to be born into a different race or nation or with skin of a different color.

In their efforts to help any possible good to become actual—either in themselves, or other persons, or a group, or community, or nation—followers of a religious path may use any means their ingenuity may devise, so long as the characteristics of their actions are religious; so long, for instance, as their actions are open, honest, thoughtful, patient, kind, generous, free of self-interest. However lofty the ends might be, the means a religious person can use must have the characteristics that are accepted, after reflective and devotional meditation, as being in harmony with what is true and good and revered as Sacred. As followers of a religious path experiment with their ability to choose the characteristics of their actions they discover that one of the given realities of human existence is that the characteristics of the action determine the results, the end, the goal—that the results may be quite different from what was anticipated or intended, what seemed to be wise, what was socially acceptable at that time and place. As they walk the religious path they discover that they are responsible for the way they walk, for the characteristics of their actions, and must accept the consequences those religious characteristics produce.

A religious pilgrim tries always to act with thoughtful awareness of the truth and the good and the Sacred. Thus, the followers of a religious path are individuals who take the initiative in developing the insights and skills that increase their ability to live harmoniously with what they have discovered to be Sacred. They try to live in harmony with the given regularities humans cannot alter in the changing circumstances where they live, and try to bring about changes in the given realities humans can modify so that some possible good will become actual.

The basic concern of a religious person is to think and act in ways that are as free as possible from self-centeredness, in ways that have religious characteristics such as patience, generosity, compassion, kindness, love. In order to have religious characteristics in thoughts and actions, the seekers use the recommended techniques for attaining tranquillity, for reflective meditation with self-examination, and for devotional meditation which is worship (alone and with others) through acts of recollection, prayer, and acts of compassionate caring. Such initiatives in developing and using religious skills continue throughout the life of each individual.

Where does the religious path go? Those pilgrims for whom the goal is to live in closer harmony with what they perceive to be true, good, and Sacred Reality, walk the path trusting that insofar as the results can be influenced by human actions they will be determind by the characteristics of their actions along the way. Teachers who give instruction about the skills needed for reflective and devotional meditation often remind religious seekers to distinguish between the techniques used and the truths discovered. Our Zen friends remind us that the way the insight comes is only the finger pointing to the moon, the religious skills are only the raft we need not carry on our back after it has carried us across the stream—after the religious characteristics that bring all actions into closer harmony with Sacred Reality have become habitual, spontaneous.

Whether the religious path is followed for only a few years or for a lifetime, along the way there will be rivers to cross, violence, accidents, pain, greed, disappointments, despair, shame, regrets—and affection, joy, happiness, moments of breath-taking beauty, and wonders pilgrims were not wise enough to seek.

Eight

Some Problems Along the Way

These reflections on problems along the way may be another example of Hakuin's monkey reaching for the moon reflected on the water.

The reflections presented here are on problems encountered and conclusions reached in my efforts, starting in the first half of the twentieth century from the perspective of an American Protestant Christian, to learn from followers of Asian religious paths how they discover and react to what they see as true, good, and Sacred. What I have accepted as true has come to me through observation and experience, verified experimentally, and modified in the light of the level of understanding attained in the changing circumstances in which my choices were made. Such conclusions run the risk of errors in dismissing some insights and practices, and in adopting others. They are open to verification and modification by anyone who wants to check them.

I have concluded that seekers can acquire the skills needed for following a religious path when they are guided by experience as it is evaluated and tested in reflective and devotional meditation. Dependable guidance for following a religious path comes from religious seekers' critical examination of what seems to be true about the given realities we can know as humans, and seems to be good and to be sacred in the world around us as observed and evaluated in our own experience and the experiences of other seekers, contemporary and in the past.

Religious experiments are made against a constantly changing background of human ignorance, indifference, selfishness, violence, cruelty, suffering, pain, worry, disappointments, remorse, and death—and of human understanding, caring, loving, affection, generosity, kindness, endurance, and joyous spontaneity. In the midst of ugliness and beauty, sorrow and laughter, of frustration and wonder, followers of religious paths have again and again discovered some dependable regularities, a sense that some insights are true and some events are good, and have become more aware of a Reality seen with awe as Sacred. Pilgrims who are guided by experience in following their path find that as they share their discoveries and insights their awareness increases, they see more clearly the religious characteristics needed along the way, and they walk their paths in closer harmony with each other and the world around them.

My observations have led me to conclude that the motivation for continuing along an experimental religious path comes from a sense of awe and reverence and gratitude inspired by glimpses of truth, of good, of beauty, and of the Sacred Power involved in the changes humans can know through reflective and devotional meditation. Such growing awareness of a Sacred Reality moving toward good through the complex, puzzling, changing realities of human experience is at the heart of a religious way of reacting to the world with trust. That trust inspires the religious seeker to continue the experimental initiative in spite of weariness and discouragement and failures.

One problem along the way for any pilgrim who

chooses to walk a religious path experimentally is that the person who experiments is part of the experiment and is altered by the experiment, and there is no way back. The characteristics of the action become the characteristics of the actor. The way a pilgrim acts determines what that pilgrim becomes. Experiments by religious seekers may be harmful or self-destructive, for instance, when the emphasis is on what the experimenter will get out of it in ecstacy or pleasure or solace or security or power or personal advantage. Or, experiments are constructive when the participants, without thought of selfish advantage, seek what is true, good, and sacred in the circumstances, thus opening the way to new religious insights and ways of acting.

When we are trying to understand the teachings and practices of the followers of Asian religious paths we discover that we must be aware of the effects in much of Asia of living under colonialism, of the barriers created between communities by self-centered exploitation, by the efforts of invading colonial powers to impose what they believed was a superior (and profitable) form of government, trade, culture, and religious practices, but was seen and remembered for generations in the "colonies" as condescending exploitation enforced by violence.

Vietnamese Mahayana Buddhists, whose explanations of their Buddhism included many Taoist and Confucian ideas, told me of the condescension they sense in Chinese Buddhists—nine centuries after Chinese domination had been overthrown. Arab Muslims often expressed similar feelings about Turkish Muslims, Sunni or Shi'i; and about the condescension, exploiting, and harsh measures used in the Arab world by European and American Christians, and by Israelis. Even after centuries, barriers raised by Islamic colonialism remain in India. Muslims in Afghanistan fear that the colonial expansion from the Soviet Union will destroy their religious community. Tibetan Buddhists, under the condescending and harsh Chinese colonial policies, fear that their Buddhism will be destroyed by the settling of millions of Chinese in Tibet. Through Asia from the Mediterranean to the Pacific sympathetic understanding between followers of different religious paths is hampered by memories of how colonial powers have shown favoritism to some paths and scorn to others.

Awareness of the ways colonial condescension has raised barriers between people makes it embarrassing to use labels like "oriental" and "occidental," "East" and "West," for specific areas of the world. East of what?—Europe?—the center from which the world is manipulated? The Near East is "near" to the major colonial powers that tried to dominate Asia; the Far East is as far east as European colonial expansion went in that direction. The center of the earth from which all else is east or west or north or south has been located by various cultures in China, India, Egypt, Makkah, Jerusalem, Athens, Rome. Now, nations with European culture put themselves there. The embarrassing claim of superiority can be lessened by using geographical names when referring to any place. The use of place names avoids the discourtesy, when in Kyoto, of suggesting to our Japanese friends that they are excluded as inferior because they live far to the east of the culture and power of Europe; or, in Damascus or Jerusalem or Istanbul that our Arab, or Jewish, or Turkish friends are Near Easterners—near, and almost in *the* West.

Often, when Asian religious teachers are asked how a seeker can make the dependable observations and evaluations needed in order to follow a religious path, they say that skill in attaining tranquillity is a necessary first step. As religious seekers become tranquil they are more at ease with themselves and the world around them, and thus better able to turn away from self-centered concerns, more open to new insights and to generous actions. Experience in developing the skills that make tranquillity possible supports the widely-held Asian conviction that the mind and body are so intimately related that it is misleading to try to deal with them separately. Thus, the religious seeker who is starting to follow a religious path is encouraged to eat some foods and avoid others, to maintain a balanced schedule of rest, and to practice regularly exercises of body and mind designed to foster such health and calmness as is possible in the circumstances.

Health, which is living in as much harmony as possible with oneself, others, and with the realities of human existence, may be sought in order to follow a religious path, to be able to be more aware of what is true and good and Sacred, and to live more harmoniously in the light of that awareness. The ability to improve and adjust to changes in one's health, and therefore to be more tranquil, is only one of several skills needed in order to follow a religious path.

The search for tranquillity creates problems for pilgrims if it becomes an end in itself, a self-indulgent pleasure, or a form of therapy for oneself and others, or an occasion for pride in one's skill in becoming tranquil. When pilgrims seek tranquillity to escape from tension, fear, illness, or pain, or to gain health, security, or peace of mind, they have chosen a bypath in an attempt to manipulate the religious way for selfish advantage.

Problems also arise in the search for tranquillity when, as Asian friends from different traditions point out, regrets for acts of cruelty, or indifference, or lust, or greed, or indolence, and the like, make it almost impossible to attain the tranquillity needed for following a religious path. The search for tranquillity raises the question as to why some ways of thinking and acting should be avoided and other ways encouraged. Is the reason for trying to act in ways that are seen as good simply that it makes it possible to follow a religious path? possible to observe and evaluate more accurately? possible to be more aware of what is true and good? possible to care, to share, to love, to pray, to worship? Many followers of religious paths would, on the basis of their experience, answer, "yes."

As they are trying to become more skillful in attaining tranquillity, seekers who follow a religious path begin to experiment with reflective and devotional meditation. In reflective meditation they become increasingly skillful in understanding and evaluating the religious insights they discover in writings, oral instructions, arts, rituals, and in their observations of the natural world and the ways religious pilgrims react to the realities in their changing environment.

In devotional meditation, as pilgrims become more skillful in prayer, worship, and in acts of caring concern in the circumstances where they live, they begin to turn from selfish concerns to a clearer awareness of what they see as true, as good, as Sacred. They discover that the characteristics of their thoughts and actions (whether they be compassionate or harsh, for instance) determine their ability to live in closer harmony with what they recognize as true, good, and Sacred.

The most pressing problems religious seekers face along the way are concerned with how to develop the personal characteristics that make it habitual to think and act in ways that are in harmony with the religious insights they have accepted as true.

Seekers who dare on the basis of experience and observation to choose how they will follow a religious path must face the surprise and dismay of others who are committed to different insights and practices they hold to be essential for any religious path. Seekers who are guided by reflective and devotional meditation as they try to help possible good become actual face the problem of how to avoid distracting controversies with others who are committed to their guidance from revelations or traditions.

Problems arise when followers of a path make choices among the cherished insights and practices of several religious paths (including their own), ignoring some, laying some aside for possible later consideration, modifying and then adopting others.

Some of my biases concerning persistent problems for followers of religious paths are shown in what has been ignored. I ignore, for instance, miracles. I am not alone in that. When I was editing a book on Islam I showed each writer what the others had written and one of them strongly objected to what another distinguished scholar wrote about miracles as proof of the truths taught by Muslims, and urged that I delete all references to miracles so the readers would not be distracted from crucially important Qur'anic teachings. (I share his opinion, but millions of Muslims would disagree with us). I ignore miracles because an event that is called unique often turns out to be seen as miraculous through ignorance or misapprehension, and because I am unable to understand how miracles prove anything to be true or good.

I ignore astrology, even though many of my friends make their decisions on the basis of astrological predictions, because I have never been able to observe any influence of stars on human conduct. I ignore amulets, and relics, when they are said to provide protection or good fortune, for I have never seen any evidence that they do. I ignore spirits, whether of plants, animals, ancestors, demons, or lesser deities, because I have never found evidence of their reality. All of these are outside my limited experience and seem to me to be minor bypaths distracting sincere seekers from the religious path they have chosen to follow. I ignore claims that secret rituals or powers can satisfy selfish desires, or can control natural processes, or material objects, or spirits, or deities—particularly when those claims are made for financial gain (as from astrology) or as a means of manipulating people for one's own purposes.

I tend to avoid use of such words as "eternal," "universal," "perfect," "absolute," "infinite," "transcendent," simply because they seem to reach out farther than my experience takes me, and I do not understand what they mean in a religious sense. I do not use the word "spiritual" because it carries so many meanings, including pride in religious accomplishments and distinctions between mind and body that I find misleading. I am uncomfortable with "idol," or "myth," even when used with careful definition lest they seem to belittle what another person sees as sacred. While I am quite comfortable to use the word "God," I find that its connotations for friends following other paths are sometimes confusing, and have therefore used "Sacred Reality" hoping it will be more widely understood as the mysterious power experienced as Sacred by the followers of several different religious paths—even though the Sacred Reality is seen from a variety of perspectives, and is described and worshiped in different ways.

In addition to *ignoring* and *avoiding*, as I studied the various forms of Hinduism, Buddhism, Islam and other Asian religious paths, I concluded that some teachings and practices could be *laid aside* for later consideration, as of secondary religious significance—even though it is quite unlikely that my friends following those paths would agree. I have laid aside revelation, salvation, soul, existence before birth and after death, heavens and hells, and mantras when they are seen as powers that alter reality.

Revelations pose a problem for anyone open to the possibility of learning from followers of different religious paths when, for example, they are presented as sacred truths to be accepted without question because they have been given from divine sources and transmitted by revered persons. Who among us can adjudicate between the revelations received by friends we like and admire: by Muslims from Allah through Muhammad, by Hindus from Brahman through Rishis, by Jains through Jinas, by Jews from God through Moses and the Prophets, by Christians from God through the Prophets and Christ—or the enlightenment that comes to Buddhists through the Buddhas and Bodhisattvas? Who can discern that one statement is a message directly from Sacred Reality while another is merely a human construct? Insofar as it is a revelation, given and transmitted by a supernatural power or being, it is impossible and would be impertinent for a human to analyze its truth or relevance, so I must lay it aside as revelation since I find myself quite incompetent to judge that one sacred teaching has been revealed and another has not.

Salvation as a problem is laid aside because it is a self-centered goal, a distracting obstacle on the path. It is self-centered either as an effort to escape from misfortune or unpleasant consequences or an effort to gain advantage for oneself such as happiness or peace of mind. Sometimes salvation is sought through self-realization, through centering attention primarily on oneself, on one's health, one's pleasures, one's talents, on the impression one is making, or on gaining power to control other people. Sometimes the salvation sought is bliss, or ecstacy, now or after death. The selfishness of such fear of misfortune or desire for self-satisfaction makes those who seek such salvation susceptible to distractions that often lead down bypaths to disillusionment.

Questions about salvation can be laid aside as irrelevant by those who see the religious way as a growing awareness of the Sacred and a continuing search for the harmony that comes through reacting with religious characteristics to the realities of human existence. When salvation is laid aside because it is seen as a self-centered goal and therefore an obstacle on the path, it raises questions leading to laying aside several related religious teachings: is a soul a reality? does an individual acquire merits and demerits, then face inevitable retribution or blessings in hell or heaven through a day of judgment or through transmigration or rebirth?

Many followers of religious paths know souls, through revelation, as unique immaterial realities, associated with a body at birth, continuing as disembodied realities after death, subject to rewards and punishments according to the choices made during their embodied existence. Sometimes souls are described as the spirits of ancestors, or as benevolent or malevolent spirits, continuing to exist for a few generations, or longer; known through human experience. Since I cannot distinguish between revelations, and in spite of my efforts have no experience that can be identified as the presence of a soul (as variously described in different traditions), I have been unable to say whether souls exist or are imaginary—I can only lay aside whatever is said about souls and get along as well as possible without knowing if they are real.

For the same reasons, I must also lay aside as beyond my ability to observe or experience: transmigration or rebirth or judgment of souls, or heavens or hells where rewards or punishments might be realized.

Followers of many religious paths are taught that while a soul is embodied here on earth good acts will be rewarded and evil acts will be punished, either in the present existence or after death. Those followers who expect only one embodiment on earth (most Muslims and Christians) anticipate a divine judgment after death with just rewards or punishment for each soul. Those who share the Hindu traditional teaching—that souls transmigrate under the just causal consequences of karma from bodily existence to bodily existence—see divine justice rewarding and punishing by the inevitable nature of each subsequent existence until release from transmigration is attained. Buddhists who accept the Buddha's teaching that souls do not exist see merit rewarded and evil punished justly in the continuing sequence of rebirths which are the inevitable consequences of thoughts and actions in previous embodied or disembodied existences. It is a sequence that continues until all causes have been eliminated—a sequence of existences I have been unable to observe or experience, so must lay aside for now as beyond my comprehension.

Heaven or hell are described as places where disembodied spirits exist. For some followers they are the places where divine judgments are made and each soul receives rewards or punishments according to the merits or demerits acquired on earth. In China, heaven is sometimes spoken of as if personified, a dispenser of justice, or at least of rewards and punishments. Other religious seekers tell us there must be hells and heavens where souls will have temporary abodes when transmigrating from bodily existence to bodily existence, or where souls exist eternally in bliss or in agony after judgment. For Buddhists, the various heavens and hells are described as places in which existence may occur from time to time as is determined by good or evil actions, so long as the round of rebirth continues. I find that I must lay aside whatever is said about heavens or hells because whatever is said about them comes from revelations, and I cannot say a revelation is true or false.

Also laid aside for later consideration is the mantra as a power that alters reality, protects from misfortune, brings good fortune, influences the Sacred. Half a century ago, when I first asked about mantras, I was told that without them there would be no religion, that the only way a human can approach the Sacred is by using this sacred sound that is the ladder reaching up to God, the rope of sound by which ascent to God is possible. I was told that a mantra—whether spoken or thought, whether a syllable or word or verse, or a musical sound, or a gesture—is a power that can only be received from a guru, person to person; that gurus who have mastered the power of the mantra can alter and transcend the given realities in the world about them, can communicate directly with other humans at a distance, can pass on the prayers of their followers to the realm of the Sacred, can compel Gods to respond favorably and to avert misfortunes that would otherwise come to humans. The effect of the mantra comes from the sound itself, not the meaning attached to it, and it must be in the original Arabic, or Persian, or Sanskrit, or Pali, or Tibetan, or Chinese, or Japanese in order to have its power. It must be uttered with complete trust and confidence.

I have listened to the chanting of mantras considered to have powers to influence events or deities, but have never been able to observe any evidence of the efficacy of the sounds other than as expressions of petition, devotion, and affirmation. I hear the Tibetan *Om mani padme hum* as a

petition for protection and an affirmation of trust; the
Shinshu *Namu Amida Butsu* as "I devote myself to Amida
Buddha;" the Nichiren *Namu Myoho-renge-kyo* as "I devote
myself to the Lotus Sutra;" the Saivite *Ci-va-ya-na-ma* as an
expression of adoration to Shiva. And I know that for my
friends who are repeating those mantras I have missed the
point when I hear their mantras as reminders, as expressions of devotion, but fail to recognize them as mantras of
power. So I have laid aside mantras of power—just as I have
laid aside revelation, salvation, soul, transmigration, rebirth, heavens and hells—as interesting speculations that
can be postponed for later consideration.

Thus, I have found that some problems along the religious path may be ignored as only minor impediments,
some must be avoided as self-centered or beyond the reach
of human experience, and some may be laid aside (walked
around?) as interesting and imaginative speculations that
distract and delay the religious search. That still leaves many
problems to be faced by pilgrims who choose to follow a
path experimentally as far as is humanly possible, and to
try to live in harmony with what they discover. These are
problems that are difficult to ignore or lay aside, problems
that may obscure the religious path or may present tempting bypaths until acceptable solutions have been found.

When I have laid aside a revelation (whether in my
own tradition or another) I often pick it up again as a human
insight worthy of careful consideration, recognizing that
neither the truth nor the error of an insight is established
by the way it has come to us, or by the number of people
who have accepted it, or by the person who presents it,
whether in words, or arts, or acts. I am aware that when
religious insights are associated with a revered scripture, or
myth, or ritual, or person (or institution, nation, or place,
or art), it may seem disloyal or arrogant or disrespectful to
entertain doubt or to insist on critical examination, evaluation, and testing. Aware, also, that pilgrims who choose to
follow a religious path experimentally by evaluating and

testing religious insights in reflective and devotional meditation reach conclusions they trust as true, with the usual risk of human error.

When revelations are examined as if they were only human insights, it becomes apparent that they differ in what they tell us is true about the nature of the Sacred, about the realities of human existence, and about possible human reactions to the world as it can be known through experience. It also becomes apparent that however these religious teachings have come to us, they have been treasured for centuries as worthy of serious consideration because of the inspiration and guidance they have given to devout seekers. Pilgrims who are following an experimental religious path have found dependable guidance when writings and works of art presented as divine revelations have been studied as human insights subject to critical analysis and acceptance as true or false.

Problems arise whenever Sacred Reality is spoken of as a Person, as Ruler, Warrior, Father, Mother, or as Creator, Controller, Judge—or as the Sacred in human form. Metaphors, imaginative stories (myths), and works of art create problems when they are accepted as factual descriptions. The limitations of attachment to a particular personal form of the Divine become more apparent when we observe different religious traditions and are told that dependable religious insights come only to those who see Sacred Reality in the personal form they have accepted. When the Sacred is known as a Divine Father or Mother or King or Judge, or as an Avatara or Incarnation or Bodhisattva, any questions we ask about what seems to be divine vengeance or neglect or favoritism become embarrassing queries about a revered Person held in high esteem. Questions about whether the Deity is male or female or androgynous are resented as flippant. After puzzling over these problems, I have come to the conclusion that in reflective and devotional meditation religious seekers who prefer to think of Sacred Reality as having personal qualities are in danger of limiting the

Sacred to their favorite metaphors and myths, in danger of distortion when they think their insights expressed in traditional personal metaphors describe Sacred Reality accurately, completely.

There are difficult problems if Sacred Reality is seen as a Creator, Controller, and Judge who has a divine plan for everything created, whose will dominates everything that happens, including the punishments and rewards given to all living things. Was the world created for the benefit of humans? Does everything happen to each individual exactly as the Creator intended, as the Controller wills: birth and death, sickness and health, talents, failures, ugliness or beauty, poverty and wealth, accidents and good fortune, famines, bountiful crops, earthquakes, floods? Are wars started, won, or lost according to the divine plan? Can humans know the plan, the will of the Creator and Controller? Can that controlling will be influenced by human actions, altered by intercessory prayers? What are the possible human choices in such a world? Are the punishments to be endured and the blessings received by humans distributed by the Controller-Judge with unfailing justice?

These are self-centered questions growing out of the metaphor of the Creator and Controller having personal qualities, including likes and dislikes that humans might be able to influence for personal advantage through rituals, sacrifices, gifts, petitions. Over the years that I have been observing people following different religious paths, I have been uneasy when they are sure they know God's plans, God's will, what God thinks, what God wants, what the Creator and Controller of the world has done and will do. Too often, the divine will turns out to be what they consider to be to the advantage of their nation, their community, their family, their religious sect, or themselves. Pilgrims along the way pose problems we cannot solve when they describe the Sacred Reality we have dimly seen as a Person whose will humans can know.

Early in my study of Asian religious ways I found that

some informants who avoided claiming to know what a Divine Controller thinks called their view of how things happen "karma." Karma, literally "action," is a widely-held view that humans can observe given regularities in the interplay of causes and effects in all aspects of human experience, in thoughts and desires and emotions as well as in the more obvious changes studied in the physical sciences. Karma, as a description of causes and effects observed, includes discovery of the good in addition to the true, recognizing that good causes have good effects. Knowledge gained by such observations comes slowly, is incomplete, may often be in error but can be checked by further observations, and has been found by many religious seekers to be trustworthy. The guidance for following a religious path comes from observing that actions having what are judged to be good characteristics can have predictable results with similar characteristics. Pilgrims who are guided by what diligent seekers have discovered in the past, and by what their own best efforts may discover in this lifetime, can help some possible good to become actual along the way.

Karma, as the recognition that there are discoverable causes and effects in all aspects of human experience, seems to me to be a dependable guide for following a religious path when the observations and evaluations are open to correction by reflective and devotional meditation. When, however, what is said about good causes and effects is extended to existences before birth and after death through transmigration or rebirth, or to assurances that the good will inevitably prevail, I have to lay such interesting speculations aside as tempting bypaths for religious pilgrims.

Some seekers say they were misdirected when told that the religious path can only be recognized by those who know what should *not* be done, and who therefore concentrate on not being greedy, nor jealous, nor proud, nor cruel, nor violent, nor fearful, nor angry; on not hating, nor lying, nor worrying—and the like. Efforts centered on *not* performing any acts with those characteristics are as futile, a

Swami friend suggested, as trying to shake a pan of sand without thinking of the word "hippopotamus." Seekers fail, the Swami said, when they concentrate on what they will *not* do because they inevitably become fascinated by evil—for it is an observable fact of human existence that "what we hate we imitate." We respond to anger with anger, to violence with violence, we hate those we think hate us; we execute murderers, we spy, we deceive, we engage in covert activites and arms races—saying we are only imitating people we have been taught to hate. Over the years, I agree with the pilgrims on many different paths who said that seekers wander down a bypath when they concentrate on what not to do, a bypath diverting them from the religious way they have chosen to follow.

Concern about what not to do raises problems about the need for purity in order to follow the path. Purity as a goal often leads to efforts to become pure by what one does not eat, nor drink, nor wear, by trying not to be afraid, nor angry, nor lazy, nor envious, nor cruel. Purification rituals that emphasize obstacles to be avoided center attention on one's self and often generate self-righteousness and ostentatious pride in what has not been done. When asceticism is practiced to obtain purity or merit or advantage for oneself, it can become an engrossing distraction; it may lead to exhibitionism; what appears to be a short-cut turns out to be a bypath.

Following negative bypaths leads to neglect of more important matters such as growing in devout awareness and acting in ways that help possible good to become actual. Beginners who are learning the art of juggling concentrate on throwing the balls in a curve that always returns to the same place, so the catching becomes automatic. Beginners who follow a religious path concentrate on acting so the results will be good in the circumstances. Thus their religious characteristics develop spontaneously.

The Jains, who discovered that the use of restraints to overcome human evil tendencies will always fail in the long run, taught that as religious seekers acquire skill in acting with outgoing compassionate concern, their self-interest and their disgust wither away unnoticed. About the same time, Chuang Tzu commented on the futility of the negative approach with this parable:

> Once there was a man who was afraid of his shadow and hated his footprints, and so he tried to get away from them by running. But the more he lifted his feet and put them down again, the more footprints he made. And no matter how fast he ran, his shadow never left him, and so, thinking that he was still going too slowly, he ran faster and faster without stop until his strength gave out and he fell down dead. He didn't understand that by lolling in the shade he could have gotten rid of his shadow and by resting in quietude he could have put an end to his footprints. How could he have been so stupid![46]

Like Rabi'a, whose love of God gave her no time to hate the Devil, the pilgrim whose actions have positive religious characteristics gains freedom from hatred of evil. The positive opposite of greed is generosity; of jealousy is caring; of violence is kindness; of hate is love; of fear is understanding; of anger is patience; of lying is honesty; of worry is hope. These opposites are some of the characteristics of a follower of a religious path. The pilgrims who after reflective and devotional meditation diligently try to think and act in ways that are generous, caring, kind, gentle, understanding, patient, loving, honest, trusting, and the like, find that desires for selfish advantage wither away through neglect. They see the path more clearly and live more consistently in harmony with what they discover to be true, good, and Sacred, without expending time and energy in discovering what not to do, and trying not to do it.

There are also problems created by religious groups, organizations, sects. Most followers of religious paths find that participation in an organized group of religious seekers provides valuable assistance to individuals and strengthens the group as they share their experience and try to put their religious insights into practice. Pilgrims along the way join with other followers in repeated rituals of learning, worship, and caring acts because together they turn from self-centeredness and increase their awareness and understanding and commitment, because awareness of the Sacred often comes when worshiping with other seekers.

Religious pilgrims, like other animals and even the plants, adjust to their changing environment and prefer congenial and familiar surroundings—such as are provided by groups of like-minded followers of a religious path. That urge to adjust, however, exposes individuals who are committed to a group to the danger of manipulation by leaders who give first place to uniformity and group strength. For instance, ritual repetition of words or phrases combined with postures and bodily movements in unison (as in a mosque or temple) are powerful means for strengthening a sense of common understanding and purpose in religious groups, and also for manipulating crowds in stadiums, military formations, parades, and riots. Group pressures can be sectarian, traditional, nationalistic, social, or may be cultural preferences for language, food, clothing, scriptures, rituals—pressures which can be as difficult to resist as addictions.

Some religious groups insist that anyone who joins with them in following their religious path must submit to a guru, a teacher, a guide recognized as having superior religious powers. Pilgrims who follow a path experimentally must decide whether they will join a religious group that requires them to submit to a guru, and if so, which guru. When I have observed a religious group following a guru who expects special recognition and submission, I have been uneasy about the harm submission to a guru does to the disciples, and the harm the disciples do to their guru by their servile adoration and obedience that encourage in the guru undue self-esteem. It has seemed to me that a religious pilgrim is wandering down a bypath when the attention is centered on the teacher rather than the teachings; or when the teachings are accepted as true because they come from a particular person; or when submission to a person is considered to be a guarantee of the truth or goodness of religious insights. The religious insights may be seen with reverence, but the person through whom they come is still only a teacher, a fellow pilgrim.

A pilgrim's relations with a group also pose the question: should the follower of a religious path set a good example? As they make their way along the path, pilgrims will gladly share what they have discovered that seems to them to be true, share their joy in what they find to be good and beautiful, and their wonder at what they recognize as Sacred. But when, if they compare themselves with others, they think of themselves as in any way superior, as able or needing to set a good example by what they do, they have turned aside down a self-centered bypath which must be abandoned if the pilgrimage is to continue. Followers of a religious path avoid that bypath of setting an example of superior wisdom or virtue when they simply try to act in ways that are caring, considerate, intelligently aware, harmonious, reconciling, creative of such good as is possible in the circumstances—without considering their reputation or image.

In the normal course, when religious pilgrims participate in groups, whether religious or secular, they find that problems arise concerning acceptable ways for the group to act. Followers of a religious path who are committed to actions having religious characteristics tell us that the religious characteristics for the actions of groups, whether informal or institutionalized, are the same as for individuals, whatever the wider social pressures for conformity might be. The actions of the family, the school, the religious organization, the corporation, the profession, the government, can also be characteristically kind, considerate, patient, honest, aware, and openly working for the good of everyone involved. The harmony of the religious way, they tell us, starts with the insights of the individual seekers, is motivated by their wonder at glimpses of the

Sacred, and comes into being when actions of individuals, alone or in a group, have religious characteristics that bring about such good results as may be possible in the changing circumstances of human existence.

Problems are created for the followers of religious paths as they discover that in the groups to which they belong by birth or by chance there are barriers between people due to the conviction that where there are differences—of color, race, gender, customs, class, education, wealth, power, religion, nationality—one's own familiar way is superior, and therefore whatever is different is inferior and may be excluded. Exclusion may be from a family, an informal group, a club, a community, an organization, an institution, a nation. Exclusion in human society is a religious problem when it is motivated by a sense of superiority, by pride, disgust, ignorance, indifference, fear, self-interest—all of which are opposites of religious characteristics. It is a special problem for pilgrims who are trying to see to it that inclusive religious characteristics shape their actions.

Organized religious communities have for centuries played a disturbing role in society through followers who accepted the teachings of a divine person or scripture or cherished tradition as superior to all other claims to know what is true and what is good. That sense of religious superiority can be dangerous and cruel, as is shown by the religious wars and social exclusions caused by aggressive efforts of Hindus, Buddhists, Muslims, Sikhs, Christians, Jews, and other religious groups to propagate or defend their superior religious community and the political organizations and social customs associated with it.

Efforts to convert create problems in the relations between different religious groups when they are stimulated by a sense of superiority. Followers who limit their religious group to their descendants, or who try to win converts from another path, create barriers between religious seekers by claiming superior and exclusive religious insights, and sometimes by belittling the practices and wisdom of the other way. Such efforts are a continuing source of friction between religious traditions and between sects within a tradition. Religious seekers who have pride in the superiority of their own religious way, to which all others must come in order to know what is true and good and sacred, often become aggressive in their efforts to convert, and are in danger of being manipulated by religious or ethnic or nationalist leaders. When devout pilgrims are trying to convert other seekers, although they are usually unconscious of the effect of their efforts, the characteristics of their actions are often seen as arrogant, or condescending, or self-centered, or manipulative. On the other hand, pilgrims who have freely chosen to move from one organized religious community to another because they find there what they accept as true and good, often help to lessen the self-centered barriers that grow up between religious groups.

The study of different paths leads to the discovery of how much devout religious seekers have borrowed from each other without moving from one religious community to another, and how today, with new ease of travel and communication, such adoptions are increasing rapidly. The spread of Hindu yoga meditation techniques throughout Asia among Buddhists and Sufis is a well-known example of borrowing. Islam in Indonesia is blended with religious practices from native religions, Hinduism, and Buddhism. Tibetans are quite aware of their selection of Theravada as the preparatory discipline for Buddhism, with the next step Mahayana, and Tantra as the highest—all selected after careful consideration. And many Tibetans recognize that the traditional Bon religious ways have also played an important role in shaping Tibetan Buddhism as it is cherished and practiced today. In Vietnam a devout Buddhist layman once explained to me what he considered to be the essence of the Buddhist Path, in words that would be completely in harmony with the *Tao-te-ching*. He had known Taoist writings from his boyhood but did not think of his Buddhism as modified by Chinese thought.

In Japan, with Shinto as a base they have borrowed Confucian and Taoist teachings and Buddhism in several different forms. Once at the home of a Soto Zen priest, when he offered me a glass of beer I replied that I could join him as his guest only if he wanted a glass himself, which he did. He smiled when I asked how he, a recognized Buddhist leader, could drink beer when the Five Precepts of Buddhism forbid alcoholic beverages, and he replied, "Ah, you should know, Buddhism did not come to Japan until it became Japanese Buddhism." Some Japanese chose to put their trust in Amida Buddha and the repetition of the Nembutsu; others put their trust in Nichiren and the *Sutra of the Lotus of the Wonderful Truth*; others became followers of Zen in the tradition of Rinzai. My host was committed to Soto Zen as taught by Dogen and his followers, having found that, for him, Soto Zen is the most helpful guide for life in the twentieth century.

In addition to the problems each religious group has in its relations with other religious organizations there are the persistent problems of the relations of religious groups with the local community, the government, and increasingly with other cultures and nations. Within each community are the problems of education, housing, health, jobs, finances, crime, and discrimination on the basis of sex, color, race, age, poverty, wealth, and social classes. Between the communities are the problems of mutual help and of exploitation and war—all raising questions as to how the actions of groups can be shaped by the characteristics to which the followers of a religious path are committed. This is the problem of ahimsa, of wu-wei, of the Tao, of the characteristics of the actions of any group with which a religious pilgrim is associated.

Pilgrims who follow a religious path experimentally face additional problems when they evaluate the differences and similarities of several religious communities. A Swiss writer chose for his book the felicitous title, *French Clocks Run Differently*. So, happily, do Shi'i and Sunni clocks, and

Vedantist clocks, and Taoist clocks, and the meditation clocks called dhyana in India and Sri Lanka, Ch'an in China, Thien in Viet Nam, and Zen in Japan. Those who have made the delightful discovery that religious clocks run differently in Makkah, Teheran, Varanasi, and Kyoto realize that even though they grew up knowing how to tell time in Jerusalem or Rome or New York, they gain new insights by learning how people respond when their clocks run differently. As they evaluate the sacred writings, rituals, and social actions of the followers of other paths, they turn back to evaluate their own by the same criteria, and find that they try to remember always to speak of a religious path other than their own as if a good friend who follows that path were present.

Seekers who hope to learn from different religious paths need to be alert to the problems created by using broad generalizations, however attractive. When a sentence starts, "All Muslims...," or "All Jews...," or "All Buddhists...," we may rightly anticipate bigotry or ignorance. Those of us who have been sufficiently identified with a religious group to be aware of the variations found in one's own community recognize the possibilities for error in such generalizations. Broad generalizations often attract attention, provoke discussion, sell publications, and create disciples. But in the study of religious paths, we should use them reluctantly, sparingly, and only after doing everything possible to substantiate them—lest they impede further understanding, and raise rather than lower the barriers between religious groups. At any rate, the making of generalizations should be preceded by the study of the many specifics in different religious ways—such as persons, places, arts, religious writings, and their consequences—and then the generalizations should be checked with followers of the path they are describing.

Like generalizations, comparisons of the differences and similarities in religious groups run the risk of encouraging a sense of the superiority of one's own path, of impeding understanding between people of different cultures. Many years ago the leaders of the Japanese Shingon sect gave a classic example in their comparative ranking of religious sects: the lowest is the animal level concerned with satisfying the desires of the belly and sex organs; then comes reliance on rules and ritual as in Confucianism; then the desire for supernatural powers as in Taoism; and up through the discovery of karma and how to escape it in Theravada; then to the higher levels of speculative accomplishments in the Hosso, Sanron, Tendai, and Kegon Buddhist sects—until the highest level is reached, which is Shingon, where the comparison started. It is this tendency to use comparisons to try to establish one's own perspective as superior that makes them suspect, whether in religious, or social, or political groups.

Comparisons can be judged on how accurately they represent the religious paths considered, how openly the biases of the persons making the comparison are stated and to what extent religious characteristics have shaped the whole process. Comparisons of religious similarities and differences may be an interesting diversion while walking a religious path and may broaden understanding when care is taken to describe and evaluate accurately without exaggeration or condescension, but comparisons serve only as an experimental technique to be used sparingly in preparation for meditation, worship, and acts of compassion.

As pilgrims who are following their path experimentally come to understand the differences between religious groups, they see that many of the differences are derived from underlying convictions about what is true and what is good in the given realities that affect human possibilities. For instance, for many Hindus their world comes into existence from a divine source and returns to that source in cycles with a definite beginning and end; the present cycle, the Kali Yuga, is inferior and running down. For many Hindus and Buddhists, that is, for hundreds of millions of Asians, the details of our transient and frustrating human existence are controlled by the causal continuity of karma through a continuing cycle of transmigrations or rebirths, eventually to be escaped. For most Muslims, this world we know through experience and revelation was created by Allah and is controlled in all details by Allah, with humans facing, after their lifetime on earth, a Day of Judgment when they will be punished or rewarded for the way they have adjusted to the God-given realities of their existence.

Fundamental convictions concerning revelation, sacred persons, places, and rituals seem to present irreducible differences when they are held to be unique, and to be necessary for human understanding of the true, the good, the Sacred. Does religious insight come through one exclusive source (Allah, Brahman, Jehovah, the Buddha, God, the Tao)? one exclusive writing (*Vedas*, *Qur'an*, *Torah*, *Bible*, *Sutra*)? one supreme Person (Muhammad, Sakyamuni, Christ, Krishna, Abraham)? through one ritual (as authorized by Hindus, Buddhists, Muslims, Jews, Christians)? Is the most sacred place Jerusalem, Makkah, Varanasi, Lhasa, Rome? Does the claim that their fundamental convictions and their irreducible differences are unique and necessary require the followers of a religious path to exclude all other pilgrims?

When pilgrims choose to follow a religious path experimentally, guided by experience and observation and their best judgment, they discover that their path is wider than they thought and there are many other paths worthy of careful consideration, some parallel and some divergent. Encouragement for continuing the study of religious ways other than their own comes when pilgrims discover men and women who have gone quite far along a different path, whose insights concerning the Sacred and how to follow a religious path provide new perspectives on familiar problems. When, through curiosity and wonder, seekers broaden their experience and their attention is centered on discovering what is true and good, their self-interest and exclusiveness melt away. As they see more clearly the fascinating complexities of religious experience in other cultures, pilgrims who move toward harmony with all forms of life turn from pointing out differences to the appreciation of similarities.

Similarities are found in interesting variants in other paths. Among the followers of religious paths some seekers, who have experienced aspects of reality as in a mysterious way Sacred, speak of Sacred Reality as a force for life and good and harmony in the world as we humans can know it. Their ways of expressing awareness of the Sacred may be traditional or daringly original, in words or arts or actions accepted as authentic by their community. What they see as true, and what they judge to be good, is shaped by what they hold to be Sacred. As seekers are awakened and turned from self-centeredness by glimpses of Sacred Reality, they become more open and recognize a similar awareness in the actions of others who describe their insights in quite different ways.

Pilgrims who follow their path experimentally share with pilgrims on other paths the realization that seeking personal advantage is an obstacle to the religious search. They are similar in their approval of persons who are concerned with the welfare of others and of their natural environment, who are helping what is seen as possible good to become actual. Pilgrims from many paths agree that their goal is to act in harmony with what they have discovered to be true, to be good, to be Sacred. They recognize followers of a religious path by the characteristics of their actions as they move toward that goal, by characteristics which are the consequences of actions of people whose attention has been centered outside themselves. While there are variations in the characteristics recognized as religious, there is general agreement among pilgrims who follow their path experimentally that the characteristics of their actions provide a dependable measure of their abiliity to follow a religious path. Their primary concern as pilgrims is to develop the religious characteristics that make it possible to discover what is true, to distinguish what is good, to move in wonder toward awareness of Sacred Reality.

Similarities are also found in the experimental methods recommended for developing the skills needed to follow a religious path: ways of attaining tranquillity, ways of reflective analysis, ways of devotional searching and acting as a religious person. There is similarity in the emphasis on the need for diligence, patience, and sensitive awareness along the religious path which continues for a lifetime that is beset by myriad frustrations, distractions and disappointments, and enlivened by affection and awe and beauty and joy and possibilities for good.

Hakuin's monkey saw the Sacred reflected on the water as a Zen Circle—for followers of other religious paths it might be a Star of David, or Cross, or Crescent, or Dancing Natarajan, or Bodhisattva, or Buddha, or Kami, or Jina. The reflection may have been seen in the generous, caring, loving acts of other persons, or in words written or spoken, or in the discoveries of the sciences through observation and experiments, or in the beauty revealed by the arts and in the natural world around us. Those reflections are seen as sacred because of the wonder, the awe they inspire, and because they bring an awareness that in all the changes in the given realities of the world around us much that is good and beautiful is possible. With such awareness comes a sense of gratitude, of joy for the opportunity to gain greater understanding of the world around us and to participate in helping possible good become actual.

The followers of religious paths, having become aware that the realities of human existence include the Sacred, reach out for greater awareness through reflective and devotional meditation tested by caring actions for the benefit of others. By turning their attention away from themselves, they seek to develop the personal characteristics that help them verify their insights, and live in closer harmony with what is true, good, and Sacred in the realities of our day-to-day existence as humans.

When we become aware of the similarities and differences in religious paths, we discover that our paths often run parallel, that irreducible differences need not keep us apart. We find that analysis of our observed differences and similarities clarifies the standards by which we judge others and ourselves. We become aware that we share many insights and practices and community tasks, we can learn from the religious arts and writings and practices of others, and that the times when we walk along the way with a pilgrim who follows another path are some of the best times of our lives.

Notes

1. A Buddhist Student of the Hebrew Bible, *Origins of Christianity*. Calcutta: Maha Bodhi Society, 2476 B.E./1932 C.E., Pamphlet No. 17.

2. Ali ibn Abi Talib, *Nahjul Balagha, Sermons, Letters and Sayings of Hazrat Ali*, comp. Syed Ruzee, trans. Syed Mohammed Askari Jafery. Hyderabad: Seerat-Uz-Zahra Committee, 1967, p. 525.

3. *Chuang Tzu*, Ch.12, trans. Chang Chung-yuan in *Creativity and Taoism*. New York: Julian Press, 1963, p. 90.

4. [Hale White], *The Autobiography of Mark Rutherford*. New York: Jonathan Cape and Harrison Smith, 1929, p. 82.

5. *The Journey to the West*, trans. Anthony C. Yu. Chicago: University of Chicago Press, 1977, Vol. 1, p. 85.

6. *Brihadaranyaka Upanishad*, 1:10,2:3, trans. V. Raghavan in *The Religion of the Hindus*, ed. Kenneth Morgan. New York: Ronald Press, 1953 (reprinted Delhi: Motilal Banarsidass, 1988), p. 319.

7. *Tao-te-ching*, 1,4,14,21,25,34,41., trans. Wing-tsit Chan in *The Way of Lao Tzu*. New York: Bobbs-Merrill, 1963.

8. *Chuang-tzu*, ed. and trans. A. C. Graham. London: George Allen & Unwin, 1981, p. 86.

9. *The Works of Hsuntze*, XVII:13, trans. H. H. Dubs London: Arthur Probsthain, 1928, p. 175.

10. al-Ghazali, *The Revivication of Religion*, trans. Margaret Smith in *Readings from the Mystics of Islam*. London: Luzac, 1950, p. 60.

11. Annemarie Schimmel, *Mystical Dimensions of Islam*. Chapel Hill: University of North Carolina Press, 1975, p. 46.

12. *Complete Works of Motoori Norinaga*, 4:548-49, trans. Joseph M. Kitagawa in *The Great Asian Religions*. New York: Macmillan, 1969, p. 297.

13. Rabi'a, trans. A. J. Arberry in *Muslim Saints and Mystics*. Chicago: University of Chicago Press, 1966, p. 51.

14. Rabi'a trans. Margaret Smith in *Readings from the Mystics of Islam*. London: Luzac, 1950, p. 10 .

15. Ali ibn Abi Talib, *Nahjul Balaqha, Sermons, Letters and Sayings of Hazrat Ali*, Khutba 86, comp. Syed Ruzee, trans. Syed Mohammed Askari Jafery. Hyderahad: Seerat-Uz-Zahra Committee, 1967, p. 178.

16. Khwaja Abdullah Ansari, *Intimate Conversations*, trans. W. M. Thackston, Jr. New York: Paulist Press, 1978, pp. 191, 208.

17. *Qur'an*, Surah XVI,89, trans. Mohammed Marmaduke Pickthall in *The Meaning of the Glorious Koran*. New York: Mentor, 1953.

18. *Complete Works of Motoori Norinaga*, 4 :548-49, trans. Joseph M. Kitagawa in *The Great Asian Religions*. New York: Macmillan, 1969, p. 297.

19. *Chuang-tzu*, ed. and trans. A. C. Graham. London: George Allen & Unwin, 1981, p. 83.

20. *Anguttara Nikaya*, I. 188, trans. Bhikkhu Kashyap in *The Path of the Buddha*, ed. Kenneth Morgan. New York: Ronald Press, 1956 (reprinted, Delhi: Motilal Banarsidass, 1988), p. 17.

21. *Selections From the Sacred Writings of the Sikhs*, trans. Trilochan Singh. London: George Allen & Unwin, 1960, p. 28.

22. *The Works of Huntze*, XXI,8, trans. Homer H. Dubs. London: Arthur Probsthain, 1928, p. 268.

23. Thogs-med bzang-po, *The Thirty-Seven Practices of All Buddhas' Sons*, trans. Ngawang Dhargyey, Sharpa Tulku, Khamlung Tulku, Alexander Berzin, Jonathan Landaw. Dharamsala: Library of Tibetan Works & Archives, 1975.

24. *Qur'an*, Surah II,148,158,159,172, trans. Arthur J. Arberry in *The Koran Interpreted*. London: George Allen & Unwin, 1955.

25. *The Bhagavad Gita*, II,56,57,64,71;III,19;XVI,1-3, trans. Swami Nikhilananda. New York: Ramakrishna-Vivekananda Center, 1944.

26. "The Ten Perfections" trans. Bhikkhu Kashyap, and "The Eightfold Path" trans. U Thittila, in *The Path of the Buddha*, ed. Kenneth Morgan. New York: Ronald Press, 1956 (reprinted, Delhi: Motilal Banarsidass, 1988), pp. 3, 104.

27. *Dhammapadam, An Anthology of Sayings of the Buddha*, 3,5,68,223,224, ed. and trans. A. P. Buddhadatta Mahathera. Colombo, Sri Lanka: The Colombo Apothecaries' Co., Ltd., n.d.

28. Thogs-med bzang-po, *The Thirty-Seven Practices of All Buddha's Sons* Nos. 1,3,8,11,21,36, trans. Ngawang Dhargyey, Sharpa Tulku, Khamlung Tulku, Alexander Berzin, Jonathan Landaw. Dharamsala: Library of Tibetan Works & Archives, 1975.

29. Tzongkhapa, *Steps of the Path*. From an unpublished translation by Sharpa Tulku and Khamlung Tulku.

30. Dogen, *Shobogenzo Zuimonki*, trans. Reiho Masunaga, in *A Primer of Soto Zen*. Honolulu: East-West Center Press, 1971, p. 50.

31. *The Analects of Confucius*, IV,2,4;V,15, trans. Arthur Waley. London: George Allen & Unwin, 1949.

32. *Mencius*, trans. W. A. C. H. Dobson. Toronto: University of Toronto Press, 1963, pp. 133, 139, 143.

33. *Mo Tzu*, trans. Burton Watson in *Basic Writings of Mo Tzu, Hsun Tzu, and Han Fei Tzu*. New York: Columbia University Press, 1967, p. 51.

34. *Tao-te-ching*, 8,49,78, trans. Wing-tsit Chan in *The Way of Lao Tzu*. New York: Bobbs-Merrill Company, 1963.

35. *Chuang Tzu*, trans. Burton Watson in *The Complete Works of Chuang Tsu*. New York: Columbia University Press, 1968, p. 95, 74.

36. *Chuang-tzu*, trans. A. C. Graham. London: George Allen & Unwin, 1981, p. 85.

37. *Chuang-tzu*, trans. A. C. Graham. London: George Allen & Unwin, 1981, p. 53.

38. Jalaluddin Rumi, trans. Reynold A. Nicholson in *The Mystics of Islam*. London: Routledge and Kegan Paul, 1970, p. 117.

39. Rabi'a, trans. Reynold A. Nicholson in *A Literary History of the Arabs*. London: Cambridge University Press, 1953, p. 234.

40. Jalaluddin Rumi, trans. Reynold A. Nicholson in *The Mystics of Islam*. London: Routledge and Kegan Paul, 1970, p. 69.

41. *The Bhagavad Gita*, II,56-57, trans. D. S. Sarma. Madras: Madras Law Journal Office, 1952.

42. *Tao-te-ching*, 77, trans. Wing-tsit Chan in *The Way of Lao Tzu*. New York: Bobbs-Merrill Company 1963.

43. Zenkei Shibayama, *Zen Comments on the Mumonkan*. New York: Harper & Row, 1974, p. 35.

44. Kao P'an-lung, *Recollections*, trans. Rodney Leon Taylor in *The Cultivation of Sagehood As a Religious Goal In Neo-Confucianism*. Baltimore: Scholars Press, 1978, pp. 130, 133, 138, 139.

45. Allamah Sayyid Muhammad Husayn Tabataba'i, *Shi'ite Islam*. Albany: State University of New York Press, 1975, p. 112. The Sixth Imam quotation is from *Bihar al-anwar*, XV, p. 208.

46. *Chuang Tzu*, ed. and trans. Burton Watson in *The Complete Works of Chuang Tzu*. New York: Columbia University Press, 1968, p. 348 Columbia University Press, 1968, p.348.